Curious? Embarrassed? Confused?

# Let's Talk About
# BUSINESS
# STRATEGY

Dr. Gerard L. Danford

Copyright © 2018 Gerard L. Danford

The reason so many strategies fail is because 'that's how we have always done it' (the strategy myth). Let's Talk About Business STRATEGY is a purpose-driven approach to strategy based on eleven talking points, which management can use throughout the organization. These eleven talking points will help everyone better understand the real meaning of strategy.

# TABLE OF ONTENTS

| | |
|---|---|
| LET'S TALK | 4 |
| THE LEARNING PROCESS | 5 |
| HOW TO TALK ABOUT STRATEGY | 6 |
| WHY GOOD STRATEGIES FAIL? | 8 |
| TRUST | 13 |
| SURVIVAL | 24 |
| RESOURCES | 33 |
| THE ENVIRONMENT | 41 |
| PROFIT | 51 |
| COMPETITION | 60 |
| GLOBALIZATION | 66 |
| GROWTH | 71 |
| PLANNING | 76 |
| MAKING STRATEGY HAPPEN! | 84 |

**LEADERSHIP** ............................................................................. 89

**STRATEGY TOOLS** .................................................................. 94

**TASK 6: FINAL ONLINE ASSESSMENT** ......................... 107

**CONCLUSION** ....................................................................... 108

**STRATEGY VOCABULARY** ................................................. 113

# Let's Talk

*'Strategy allows everyone to concentrate on the hear-and-now, while knowing that they are heading in the right direction'*

Only 29% of employees in organizations can correctly identify their company's strategy (Jimmy Leppert, Harvard Business Review). This sad fact suggests that there exists a large gap between employees and strategic understanding. This misalignment can result in;

- Slowing down of the entire organization (nobody knows what they do to support the strategy).
- Operating under false assumptions (not effective).
- Using up valuable energy when pursuing the wrong priorities (not efficient).
- Diluting talent (not directed towards the right actions).
- Misalignment between organizational goals (not understanding goals).

Let's Talk About Strategy helps everybody understand what strategy is, and the important role everyone plays in making a strategy successful.

# The Learning Process

Let's Talk About Strategy is structured around eleven principles (talking points). Those principles have been developed by the author after spending more than 20 years in management consulting, and 20 years teaching strategy in B-Schools. The strategy talking points are supported by the latest research. In addition to the eleven strategy talking points, Let's Talk About Strategy includes exercises, and self-assessment tools which help everyone understand the concepts covered (links to external tools allow the readers to evaluate their employer/company). At the end of Let's Talk about Strategy there is an online assessment of the content covered.

# How to Talk About Strategy

In the MINI MBA Bootcamp Book (Amazon), we introduced the four strategic styles developed by the Boston Consulting Group (BCG). Those four styles are determined by the level of predictability and the environmental conditions a company faces. The first of those two conditions (Level of Predictability), influences how far into the future and accurately a company can confidently forecast demand, performance, competition, and market expectations.

The second condition is called Malleability-Workability (to what extent a company, or their competitors, can influence the level of predictability). Based on these two variables (predictability and malleability-workability), we then constructed a four-quadrant strategy style matrix. Depending on where a company fits into the matrix, one can then determine the best strategic style. According to BCG, companies who best match their strategy style with the conditions in their business environment; have been found to out-perform others (+4% to +8% on returns).

**Note: Links to Mini MBA**

Amazon.com https://goo.gl/FrLsPP

Amazon.uk https://goo.gl/piUzaS

## Strategic Style - Agile Strategy

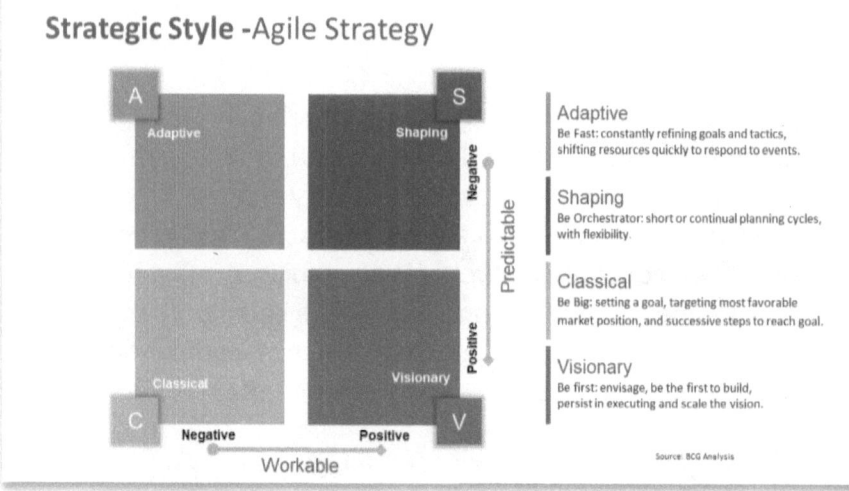

The most common strategic styles used by companies today are more suited to predictable environments (40% use visionary, 35% classical, 16% adaptive and 9% shaping). This situation is in fact a serious mistake because; most companies today are faced with highly unpredictable and fast moving environmental conditions;

1. **Classical Style**: Suitable in predictable but hard to change environments.
2. **Adaptive Style**: Suitable in less predictable and faster moving environments.
3. **Shaping Style**: Suitable in less predictable but workable environments.
4. **Visionary Style**: Suitable in more predictable and workable environments.

# Why Good Strategies Fail?

*'Strategy = Knowing where you're going, why you're going there, how you're getting there, and what's different about how you're doing it'*

The four BCG strategic styles discussed above can help a company evaluate the impact of their environment on their business strategy. Based on the assessment of that impact, companies can then select one of the 4 strategy styles. However, even if companies make the right strategy style selection, it is not uncommon for even a great strategy to fail.

A recent Economist Intelligence Unit report called *'Why Good Strategies Fail: Lessons from the C-Suite'* shows that only 44% of senior executives feel that creating an appropriate strategy is essential or very important. However, 88% of those same executives said that executing strategic initiatives was essential/very important for success to occur. This 'Great-Strategy vs. Great-Execution' chicken and egg dilemma has in fact existed for some time.

Prof. Robert. Kaplan and Prof. David Norton (Harvard Business School) have claimed already in 2005 that; '95% of a company's employees are unaware of, or do not understand its strategy, and that companies on average deliver only 63% of financial performance their strategies promise'. Therefore, we could say that a great strategy is nice to have but, lack of understanding (what is strategy?) and poor communication, are two of the primary contributors to failed strategies and performance loss in companies. This occurs because; 'without clarity and understanding of strategy, lower levels in the organization cannot put in place executable plans'.

Therefore, in order to execute a strategy successfully, it is first and foremost necessary for everyone to understand what strategy is! In Let's Talk About Strategy we will drill-down into this question and consider; how can we get every employee to understanding strategy? Understanding is essential because; when everybody understands what 'strategy' means, the likelihood of having a successful one increases. This happens because understanding strategy;

- Gives employees purpose.
- Gives employees more control.
- Helps improve individual and group performance.
- Helps employees understand why they are doing what they are doing (effort).

Strategy has been turned into a very complex subject by academics and consulting companies. However, there are in fact just eleven basic principles which everyone should understand about strategy. By understanding these eleven simple principles, everyone in any organization can better appreciate the real meaning, and importance of their organizations strategy. Those eleven principles are;

## Let's Talk Strategy Principles

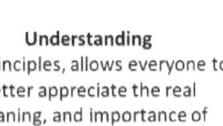

**Understanding** the principles, allows everyone to better appreciate the real meaning, and importance of strategy!

- **TRUST** (belief): Without trust, the performance of a strategy will be less than 'all it can be'.
- **SURVIVAL**: Focusing on short-term performance, neglects long-term robustness (businesses are disappearing faster than ever before).
- **RESOURCES**: Without the necessary resources; customer value, process effectiveness/efficiency, and healthy profits, will not be realized.
- **ENVIRONMENT**: Growing complexity is making it harder for companies to control the business context they live in.
- **PROFIT**: Generating greater value for the customer is the primary source of sustainable profits. Profit is the fuel and the reward for a successful strategy.
- **COMPETITION**: Without healthy competition, companies do not become 'all that they can be'. Furthermore, they will never experience the thrill and reward of winning.
- **GLOBALIZATION**: Brings with it; new players, new games (products and services), and new

playing fields (markets). 'Ignoring globalization is the same as arguing against the laws of gravity'.
- **GROWTH**: Results in adding more complexity to a business. No growth is better than un-balanced growth that lacks a clear and well-defined purpose.
- **PLANNING**: Inclusive, asks the right questions, makes the strategy real, views the environment in a new way, and brings order and direction to everyday routines.
- **MAKING IT HAPPEN**: Road blocks to success are created by not having crystal clear and understandable communication (specific goals that are driven by a common purpose).
- **LEADERSHIP**: Requires good judgement, and well-defined priorities which employees believe (trust), support (effort) and get excited about.

Before you read further, stop for a moment to think about the eleven principles listed above. Do you agree with those principles (why-why not). Is there one principal in the list which might be critical for your business (if so, why)? Finally, what might be missing from the list, but is essential to having a successful strategy?

By asking these kinds of questions, you, too, can enhance your understanding of strategy!

## SOURCES:

- Why Good Strategies Fail: Lessons from the C-Suite (2013). The Economist Intelligence Unit
- Kaplan, Robert. and D. Norton (2005). The Office of Strategy Management. Harvard Business Review
- Reeves, Martin (2015). Does Your Strategy Need a Strategy? Wharton, University of Pennsylvania
- Leppert. Jimmy (2013). When CEO's Talk Strategy, Is Anyone Listening. Harvard Business Review

# Trust

*'Trust must be earned'*

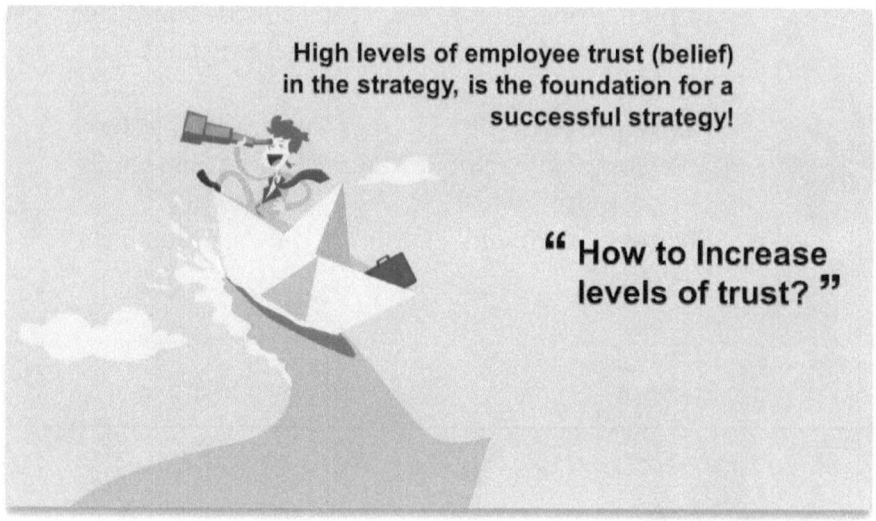

The most essential ingredient for implementing a successful strategy is trust (belief). Trust is not discussed a lot in business (why?). However, high levels of trust are critical for every social unit to prosper (significant others, families, and even businesses). When trust is absent in a business; the wishes, desires and vision of leaders, and their strategies, will always come into question. Trust (belief), is in fact, the foundation of every successful strategy! Unfortunately, the research shows that more than 50% of employees do not even trust their bosses. Have you ever asked yourself; 'do I trust (believe in) the strategy of my organization'?

## DEFINITION:

*Trust is based on four variables (credibility, reliability, intimacy and self-orientation). Trust is also a bi-lateral relationship (trust/trusted). Trusting is therefore, a byproduct of the behavior of another person based on these four variables.*

**TRUST EQUATION**

$$T = \frac{C+R+I}{S}$$

Credibility: Words we speak
Reliability: Actions we take
Intimacy: Safety/Security we give
Self-Orientation: We vs Me

Source: TrustedAdvisor Associates

The level of trust can be boosted in an organization (credibility, reliability) when management begin to recognize and understand the important contribution every employee is (or can) make in the company's strategy. This boost occurs because, when employees better understand their contribution, they are motivated to give more (increase effort and stretch). However, when employees do not understand a strategy or their personal contribution to that strategy, how can we expect them to commit the levels of trust (belief) which are going to determine the success of that strategy? If trust is absent, all that employees will feel are uncertainty, lack of control, and unwillingness to support the strategy. Trust (belief) therefore, is the foundation of every successful strategy.

When trust levels are low uncertainty occurs because; the company's strategy is leading everyone towards an unknown future. We all know that unknown is not a very nice place to find yourself every day of the workweek. However, when employees are well informed, before and during the strategy journey, they will then be able to make better decisions and give more commitment (including trust). In fact, when high levels of trust (belief) are present, employees will make more effort and accept increased risk. Therefore, management must always be conscious of the fact that; employees are making judgements on the level of trust (belief) they wish to give to leaders, managers, and strategies, all the time.

Another challenge organizations encounter when implementing a strategy is; the strategy often requires people to change their behavior. Unfortunately, changing people's behavior is easier said than done. Quite often, behavior changes will only occur if there is a crisis (a need to be punished or challenged). However, a crisis is not always necessary to change behavior in an organization.

When all employees are provided with the essential information (understanding), it is easier for them to begin to change. However, that information must show people how they will personally play a valuable (constructive) role in the company's future success. Behavior change will occur then because, when people have all the information they need, they can more easily make those difficult trust decisions (do I support the strategy enough to change my behavior?).

The answers to the above questions will determine if people are willing to give more or less 'effort' towards what is needed to succeed! However, more often than not, companies expect employees to immediately believe in the strategy, and to give 100% effort, in spite of the fact that those employees may not understand what that strategy actually means. This understanding-gap occurs when;

- The strategy has not been explained in simple and understandable language.
- The strategy has not been communicated effectively (face-to-face, up and down the organization, and frequently).
- The strategy has not been linked to individual's roles, responsibilities and effort (personalized). When there is no accountability, there is no responsibility.
- The rewards of a successful strategy have not been made clear (for every individual and the organization as a whole). Those rewards do not necessarily have to be financial.

When trying to gain the understanding of all employees, it is necessary to speak the same language. However, to arrive at a common strategy language, management must first define and agree on a common vocabulary (and meaning of that vocabulary). Over time that language will become the organizations strategic-vocabulary. It is also important to remember that the strategic-vocabulary should be simple yet understandable, and the vocabulary should have meaning.

It is no surprise that winning companies often have an agreed upon strategic language, which is clear and thoughtful. This is done because; winning companies know that relevant and understandable communication is essential for success to occur. It is essential because only then will every employee understand what is required of them, when it is required, and why it is required. Furthermore, winning companies also create a well-defined map (strategy), which shows employees where they are going, the progress being made during the journey, and the desired outcome. Because of these rather simple efforts, employees in winning companies know when to avoid the wrong alternatives (decisions and actions), which are not helping get them closer to the finish line.

Before you read further, why not stop for a moment and think about the strategic-vocabulary used in your organization. Do you understand the vocabulary? Does the strategy vocabulary help you to engage better with the company's strategy and guide you during the hundreds, if not thousands, of decisions you make every day on the job? By asking these questions (and others), you can accelerate your learning process.

At this stage in Let's Talk About Strategy please review the; 'Do Your People Understand Strategy' questions listed below. In doing so, you will be better prepared for the content we will discuss next.

# Understanding Strategy
## Ask the following questions about your organization

| | YES | NO | WHY? |
|---|---|---|---|
| Are we merely surviving? | | | |
| Do we have the resources needed to move beyond survival? | | | |
| Do the resources meet the needs of the changing environment? | | | |
| Are people capable and willing to change? | | | |
| Is competition considered to be good or bad for us? | | | |
| Does globalization frighten people? | | | |
| Is growth always considered to be necessary and good? | | | |
| Does everyone contribute to planning the future? | | | |
| Are individual and team roles/responsibilities defined precisely? | | | |
| Do leaders communicate goals, roles and responsibilities daily? | | | |
| Do people trust (believe) the strategy? | | | |

# CASE "THE HP WAY"

*The Hewlett-Packard Company (HP) was listed (#10) in the very first Fortune Magazine ranking of the '100 Best Companies to Work For' in 1998. That ranking was designed to provide a measure of employee trust.*

*The founders of HP in 1957 wrote down their management beliefs regarding; respect of and trust in employees, an environment that fosters creativity, and a flat management hierarchy. Those beliefs became known as the "HP Way", has served as a model for companies' culture.*

*In 1999 HP appointed a new CEO, Carly Fiorina (an outsider). Fiorina was a highly competitive and results oriented manager. By 2000, HP had fallen to #43 on Fortune's list. Part of that decline was due to Fiorina's claims that HP needed to; increase the sense of urgency, and develop a more competitive spirit. Fiorina also publicly indicated that she was dissatisfied with HP employees. In April 2001, HP laid off 6,000 employees. Furthermore, HP did not make the "100 Best Companies to Work For" in 2003 or 2004. In 2005 a new CEO was appointed (Mark Hurd). Hurd claimed he would follow "The HP Way", but in 2006 he fired 15,300 employees.*

**What can we learn from the HP case?**

- *Signals of; respect, fairness, satisfaction with and pride in employees, are critical to creating organizational trust among employees.*
- *The opposite signals such as; disrespect, unfairness, and dissatisfaction, may cause distrust.*

# CRITICAL QUESTIONS

To help internalize the knowledge gained in this session, consider the following questions for a company you are working with, or one you are investigating.

1. What is the companies Trust Barometer level (willingness to giving trust...earn trust)?
2. What systems are in place to support trust (knowledge, acceptable behaviors, incentives, and enforcement)?
3. Does the company communicate effectively (listen to... and heard)? If not, what could be done better?
4. Is **everyone** aware of the findings from the above questions?

# TASK 1: ARE YOU A TRUSTED LEADER?

Take this trusted leader self-assessment test now to determine how you rank on behavior, legacy, community and vitality in your organization.

LINK: The Trusted Leader Assessment
https://goo.gl/NkYW3a

Note: No registration is required

# TASK 2: WHAT IS YOUR TRUST QUOTIENT (TQ)?

Take the trust quotient quiz to learn what your biggest strengths are, and your biggest opportunities for improvement (a diagnostic report is provided).

LINK: How Trustworthy Are You? TQ Self-Diagnostic Assessment
https://goo.gl/EfSmNe

Note: Email registration is required (any email can be used: not required to confirm before taking test-getting results).

# SUMMARY

**The managerial and employee communication challenges which need to be addressed.**

## TRUST

| MANAGEMENT | EMPLOYEES |
|---|---|
| ✓ Organizational wishes, desires and vision? | ✗ Understand my/our contribution? |
| ○ Required levels of effort and stretch? | ○ Management: credibility reliability and intimacy? |
| ○ How to navigate the unknown future? | ○ My/our level of risks vs commitment? |
| ○ Reporting progress? | ○ Effort vs reward? |

## SOURCES:

- Covey, Stephen, and D. Conant (2016). The Connection Between Trust and Financial Performance. Harvard Business Review
- Financial Performance: Trust Fuels Business Outcomes (2016). Great Places to Work
- Atkins. Andy, (2014). Building Workplace Trust: Trends and High Performance. Interaction Associates
- Drapeau, A.S. and R. Galford (2003). The Trusted Leader. Center for Leading Organizations
- Edelman Trust Barometer (2016). Edelman Inc.

- Green, Charles (2007). Trusted Business Relationships: The Core Concepts. Trusted Advisor Associates
- Reeves, Martin, S. Levin, and D. Ueda (2016). The Biology of Corporate Survival. Harvard Business Review
- Elsbach, K. I. Stigliani, and A. Stroud (2011). The Building of Employee Distrust: A Case Study of Hewlett-Packard from 1995-2010. Organizational Dynamics

# Survival

*'It is not the strongest species that survive; it's the one that is most adaptable to change'*

(Charles Darwin)

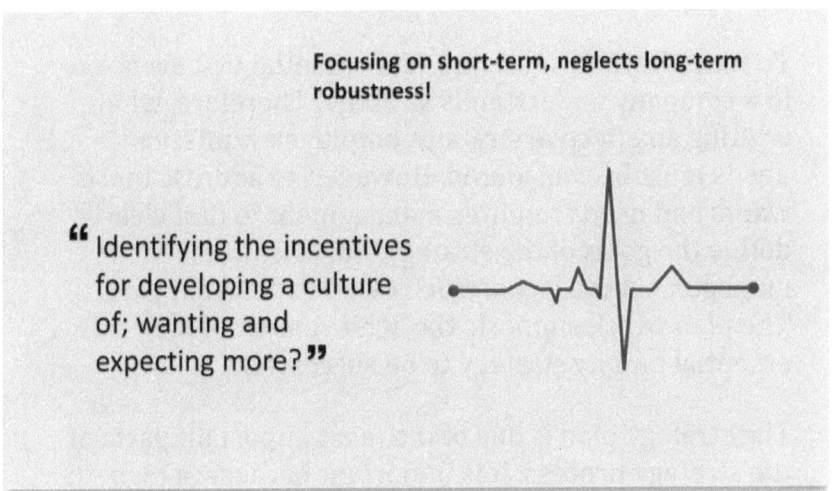

The Boston Consulting Group (BCG) has studied 30.000 public firms in the USA over a 50-year period to determine how their strategies have impacted the company's survival rates. Their findings from that research are very disturbing. They are disturbing findings because; businesses today are disappearing more rapidly than ever before. In fact, public companies today have a life expectancy rate which is lower than that of their average employee. Mortality rates of public companies are in fact rising rapidly (6x higher than 40 years ago). The main causes of this growing company mortality rate are;

- Failure to adapt to increasingly complex environments.
- Having the wrong strategy.
- Lacking capabilities and appropriate behavior.

***Do you want your company to merely survive?***

To move beyond surviving, it is essential that everyone in a company understands strategy! Therefore, when crafting an effective strategy, employee wants, and needs must be considered. However, to address those wants and needs requires management to first clearly define the goals of the strategy. Furthermore, management must construct a well-articulated plan. The plan which supports the achievement of the goals is essential for any strategy to be successful.

The strategy plan is one of the most important parts of the strategy process. It is important because; a plan which gains the support of most employees will help everyone move beyond survival. However, without a goal, which is supported by a plan all employees believe in, the company will only end up drifting in the sea. As we all know, a company drifting in the sea is not safe or secure for anyone. Therefore; if we want all our employees to feel safe, we need clearly defined and understandable goals, which are supported by a well-articulated plan. Without those building blocks (goal and plan), management cannot guide employees in the right direction (towards success).

The map to where we are going represents an import part of the strategy process. When we have an understandable map, we can regularly check the direction, and measure our progress. If the route and the destination have been planned well, employees will accept the map. If the route needs to change during the journey, employees will also be able to judge and understand those changes. The most important thing about the strategy map is that it helps employees visualize the journey and the destination (the reward for effort). However, that destination may sometimes also need to change during the journey.

When high levels of trust are present, those difficult decisions (changes in strategy), will in fact be made easier to accept. Therefore, companies must have an understandable strategy roadmap, (even if it is not perfect). An imperfect roadmap in fact, is better than having no map at all. Having a map also makes life easier for everyone. It does so because; having the map allows employees to concentrate their efforts on the right things throughout the journey. They can do this because; they don't need to spend all their days wondering where they are going (the direction of their lives and the company's life).

Unfortunately, many companies are surviving because they have not created, or agreed upon, an **understandable strategy map**. However, despite this, they think that everything is OK (because surviving is comfortable). Those companies operating without an understandable map have in fact become happy, and even satisfied with merely 'surviving'. This occurs because; survival does not always feel like a crisis. However, as with an iceberg in the sea, the danger is hidden deep below the surface. The danger is hidden because the necessary changes are not being made; the company is not renewing itself, and not investing for the future. In fact, for those companies a crisis is looming. This is happening simply because they have become satisfied with survival. Unfortunately, survival may have been enough yesterday and enough today, but it is not enough if we all want more tomorrow and in the future.

According the Maslow's hierarchy, survival is one of our most basic needs (oxygen, water, food and a roof over our head). When our basic level needs are met, we then seek safety and security. From there we seek friendships, relationships and love (a sense of belonging). When those needs are met, we may seek respect and appreciation from others (and respect for ourselves). Self-respect in fact brings with it; confidence, independence, and freedom. According to Maslow, our needs are like a pyramid. Under ideal conditions those needs should grow higher and higher, as our basic needs are satisfied. This should happen because; when people do not meet their basis survival needs, they feel dissatisfied.

The real challenge emerges when people have met their basic survival needs. This becomes a challenge because; when people have met their basic survival needs, they feel nothing more than content (not missing anything). In fact, meeting all the basic survival needs does not make people feel satisfied or dissatisfied. What this means is that; meeting our survival needs does not motivate us to make more effort to move beyond survival. This is happening because; when we are surviving comfortably, we often don't seek anything more (not missing anything). However, a company (group of people) should desire more than just survival and should strive to become 'all that they can be'.

Now, you may have thought that every person is trying to satisfy their higher-level needs. In fact, when people (and companies) are 'surviving', they are not making an effort to satisfy higher-level needs. This is the case because, when people have spent their lives just barely satisfying their basic survival needs, they ignore the need to be 'all that they can be'. However, understanding the rewards of a successful strategy is one way for employees to recognize; why it is important to care about moving beyond survival. Furthermore, a successful strategy (and the rewards it brings) helps motivate employees to make more effort. That increased effort occurs because employees wake up and begin to understand that survival isn't enough. In fact, they recognize that survival is preventing them from realizing more in their lives. This is the biggest reward from having a clearly defined, understandable and relevant strategy.

The important point to remember here is that; *when people want more, it will result in them giving more effort... in order to get more.* Having a strategy and understanding that strategy allows employees to recognize the limitations which have existed, and to see beyond those limitations. Therefore, by understanding strategy, employees realize that there is a safer and better life for them to look forward to. However, to achieve that understanding, it is necessary for management to;

- Understand the needs of the company, and all its employees.
- Articulate (clear and distinct) the strategy goals (which meet those needs).
- Craft a plan for how to achieve the goals, through the efforts of every single person.

The next essential step (after completing the above), is to consider if the organization has the necessary resources which will make the strategy successful. This next step is essential because, without those necessary resources, the organization will not survive for long, and will be unable to improve their current conditions. Not having the necessary resources in fact, is like having a fancy sports car without gasoline in the tank.

## CASE: THE LAST KODAK MOMENT

*Kodak was the Google, of the 1800's. The company was known for innovative technology and marketing. In 1976 Kodak had 90% of the film market and 85% of camera sales in America. Up until the 1990's the company was one of the world's five most valuable brands. In 2012 the company's share price dropped -90%.*

*Fuji (Japan) was in the same business as Kodak however, they recognized already in the 1980's that digital was the future. Unlike Kodak, who suffered from a mentality of 'perfect products', Fuji embraced the philosophy of; 'make it, launch it, and fix it'. Fuji also managed to diversify more successfully. The film business at Fuji in 2000 still represented 60% of their profits, but the company milked those profits and used them to develop new sources of revenue. Kodak, having survived more than 130 years, eventually 'saw the tsunami coming, but there was nothing they could do about it.'*

## CRITICAL QUESTIONS

To help internalize the knowledge gained in this session, consider the following questions for a company you are working with, or one you are investigating.

1. Have you identified, understood and defined (facts), the needs and wants of the company (employees, management, stakeholders etc.)?
2. Do you understand the limitations (barriers) to achieving those needs and wants (go and see)?
3. Have you defined the benefits of developing a culture for; wanting and expecting more (which will bring more)?
4. Is **everyone** aware of the findings from the above questions?

## TASK 3: IS YOUR STRATEGY ABOUT TO FAIL?

How likely is it that your company will fail? Take the Harvard Business School/Boston Consulting Group (BCG) test to determine the answer.

LINK: Strategy Failure Assessment (Harvard Business School)
https://goo.gl/7ZjMVG

Note: No registration is required

# SUMMARY

The managerial and employee communication challenges which need to be addressed.

### SURVIVAL

| MANAGEMENT | EMPLOYEES |
|---|---|
| ✓ Gauging status of existing culture? | Self-awareness of desires, wants, needs? ✗ |
| ○ Articulating (clear) strategic goals? | Incentive to 'desire and want' more? ○ |
| ○ Gathering data and facts (benefit of strategy)? | Recognize my/our limitations? ○ |
| ○ Creating support mechanisms (mapping progress)? | Understanding? ○ |

# SOURCES:

- Reeves, Martin, and S. Levin and D. Ueda (2016). The Biology of Corporate Survival. BCG Perspectives
- Maslow, Abraham (1943). The Theory of Human Motivation. Psychological Review
- Kutcher, Eric, O. Nottebohm, and K. Sprague (2014). Grow Fast of Die Slow. McKinsey Quarterly

# Resources

*'We have not started to live, before we rise above of our individualistic concerns'*

Martin Luther King, Jr.

We cannot have the material things we desire in life without money. We cannot build a house without resources. We cannot have a winning team without players. For all of those to happen, we need resources. Money is one resource, knowledge is another, and employees are one of our most valuable resources. Therefore, to 'be all that we can be' requires the right resources. Those resources will allow us to satisfy our needs. When we are satisfying our needs, we are also learning and discovering new things. That journey of discovery also affects the current and future strategy of every company.

Resources are the fuel for strategy, because they help companies get to the desired destination. When we combine resources in the right way, we can even achieve a; 1 + 1 = 3 result. What this means is that the whole is in fact greater than the sum of the individual parts. This is one of the rewards of having a strong, healthy and prosperous company. Healthy companies are in fact like an efficient spider's web (a useful tool to catch food). The organizational spider's web is effective when all of the members are inter-connected, and each one influences the whole in a positive way (the organization is one). How we deploy those resources however is critical and is another component of all successful strategies.

McKinsey research confirms that corporations do not effectively allocate resources (human, capital etc.) to support their strategies. This occurs despite the enormous amount of strategic planning companies' carryout. In fact, companies make moderate if no shifts in their resource allocations year after year (this is also true across different industries). However, the companies who do actively re-allocate resources as a part of their strategic initiatives achieve +30% higher return for shareholders. Furthermore, resource re-allocators are +13% more likely to avoid bankruptcy or acquisitions. The sad news for companies with low levels of resource re-allocation activity is that, their Chief Executive Officers (CEO's) are more likely to be removed from their position in a shorter period of time.

Resource allocation is also critical when a company begins to explore alternative business models (or is forced to do so). The Boston Consulting Group (BCG) has determined that 94% of companies (sample size of 1,500 executives), have attempted some degree of business model innovation in the past. This is important for us to understand because strategies often involve business model innovation, and the success of those initiatives can be directly influenced by resource allocation and resource capabilities.

Before describing findings from a recent Harvard Business School study on business model innovation and its impact on resource allocation, it is necessary to first agree on; what is a business model? A business model is made up of four elements;

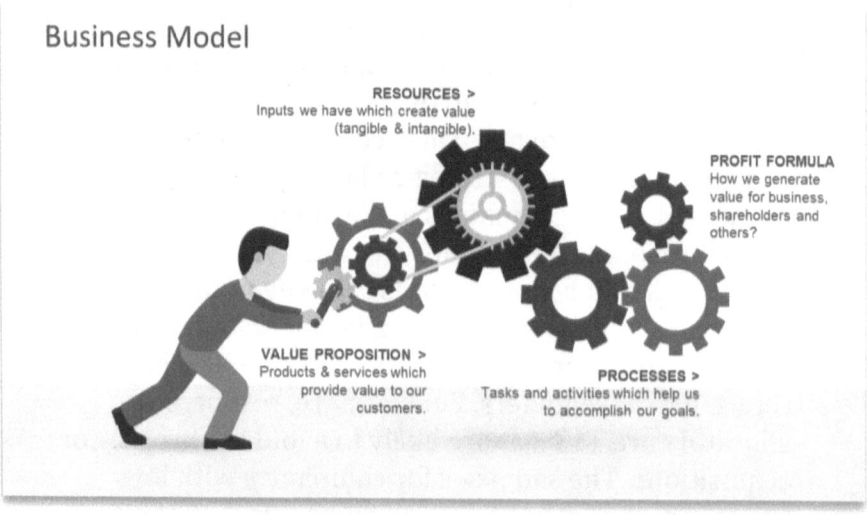

The value proposition in a business model (Harvard Business School) reflects the value-created for customers. Resources include; people, money technology and more. Processes involve those activities which convert inputs into final goods (products and services). The profit formula determines; margin, asset velocity, and the scale of the business which is needed to achieve the desired level of returns. The inter-relationships and inter-dependencies between these four elements must also be considered (to achieve the necessary levels of integration etc.).

## Business Model Elements

**PRIORITIES**

VALUE
Increase Value
For customer effectiveness, efficiency, convenience, affordability...

PROFIT
Cover Costs
Through asset allocation, fixed costs, margins, and asset-use efficiency...

**CAPABILITIES**

RESOURCES
Support Value
Through people, technology, products, equipment, brand...

PROCESSES
Optimize (effective & efficient)
Re-occurring tasks, planning, budgeting, manufacturing, training...

Source: Christensen et al (2016)

## Business Model Elements

Business models in fact become less flexible as they mature (this makes changing an established business model challenging). Furthermore, the development of a new business model can take some time. As that time unfolds, the model becomes less malleable (stage 1: new business model, stage 2: sustaining-model, and finally stage 3: efficiency-model). Therefore, when attempting to achieve successful business model innovation (resource re-allocation) it is wise to remember that;

*Creating new business models (re-allocating resources), is often more effective than attempting to change existing and well-established business models'*

A successful strategy needs the right resources, and effective resource allocation (business model). This also requires that companies are aware of the environment they live in. This is important because, matching resources with opportunities in the environment is essential for a company to survive, and to move beyond survival. Therefore, everyone must understand that the environment impacts the business, and that environment is constantly evolving and changing (the earth never stops rotating). In fact, what this means is that change is part of the world we live in. Because of this fundamental fact, everyone must be ready to adapt and change to meet the new environmental conditions they will encounter tomorrow.

# Case: Water Is the New Oil

*Most people treat water as a "free" resource. However, for some companies advanced water management is becoming more important as they aim for zero waste, maximum recycling and regeneration. Companies including Nestlé, PepsiCo, and InBev are already focusing on sustainable water management. In India, PepsiCo already returns more water to communities where it operates than it consumes.*

*For Coca-Cola water is at the heart of their business. 'inside every bottle of Coca-Cola is the story of a company that understands the priceless value of water, respects it as the most precious of shared global resources and works vigorously to conserve water worldwide'.*

*Coca-Cola sells its products mostly where they make them. If those communities stay strong, their business will stay strong. Because of this fact, Coca-Cola has a need to preserve and improve water sources. The company has a goal of being water neutral by 2020. The company also requires all of their bottling plants to conduct a source-vulnerability assessment. That assessment involves an inventory of risks to the water sources supplying their facilities and the surrounding communities. Based on those assessments, a plant-specific risk-mitigation actions plan is made for sustainability.*

## CRITICAL QUESTIONS

1. Do your existing resources meet the needs of the marketplace (games, playgrounds) tomorrow?
2. Have you defined; where, how and why your resources create value (1+1=3)?
3. Are you making the necessary investments to strengthen your resources, (where, how, why)?
4. Is **everyone** aware of the findings from the above questions?

## SUMMARY

**The managerial and employee communication challenges which need to be addressed.**

### RESOURCES

| MANAGEMENT | EMPLOYEES |
|---|---|
| ✓ Resource audit and resource allocation? | ✗ My/our capabilities and influence? |
| ○ Mapping inter-relationships and inter-dependencies? | ○ Understanding why 1+1=3? |
| ○ Defining value proposition and profit formula? | ○ My/our contribution to a positive outcome? |
| ○ Need for business model innovation? | ○ Appreciate needs of the marketplace? |

## SOURCES:

- Hall, Stephen, D. Lovallo, and R. Musters (2012). How to Put Your Money Where Your Strategy Is? McKinsey Quarterly
- Christensen. Clayton, T. Bartman and D. van Bever (2016). The Hard Truth About Business Model Innovation. MIT Sloan Management Review
- Birshan, Michael, M. Engel, and O. Sibony (2013). Avoiding the Quicksand-10 Techniques for More Agile Corporate Resource Allocation. McKinsey Quarterly
- Nyquist, Scott, M. Rogers, and J. Woetzel (2016) The Future Is Now: How to win the resource revolution. McKinsey Quarterly

# The Environment

*'Can we control our environment, or does our environment control us?'*

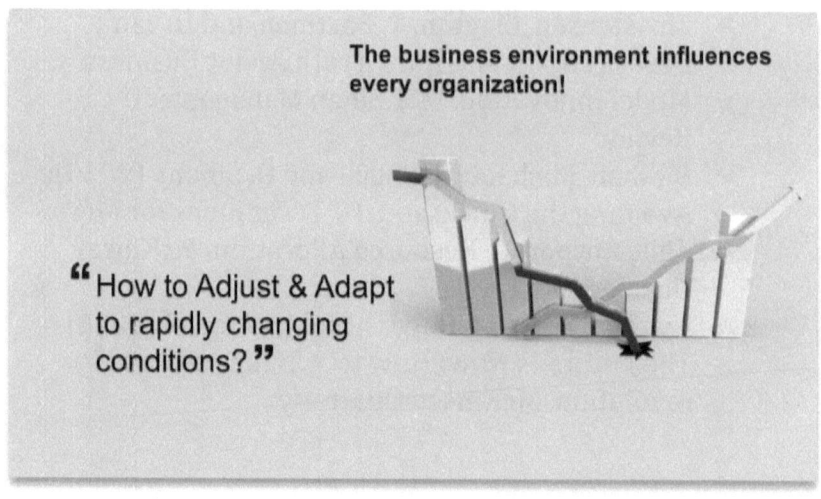

The world is changing rapidly, and there is never a moment when everything stops. Because of this constant change, it may feel like life is getting harder and harder. However, change can be both positive and negative. Therefore, we must be sensitive to, and accept change, in order that we can adapt and benefit from the positive changes occurring.

In life we can sometimes chose what playground (market) we wish to play in, and the people we wish play with. However, sometimes we must play as best we can in the playground we are given. Those playgrounds (the business environment) will have many kinds of players who might be playing different games (products and services). Furthermore, each game has different rules. Therefore, deciding which game we wish to play is an important part of every strategy. Playing the game (product and service) which fits best our strategy is the wisest choice. Selecting the right playground (markets), is even more critical. The right playground is critical because; making the wrong choices could destroy our plans. Therefore, making the right choices is essential for every successful strategy.

When we play with companies and customers who we know and understand, it feels comfortable. However, we should not let comfort prevent us from looking for a better game (products and services), or a better playground (markets). In other words, we should not allow comfort to limit our potential, and to prevent us from seeking new opportunities (despite how uncomfortable that might make us feel). This is a very important point to keep in mind because; when the games and playgrounds are changing rapidly, we can miss opportunities if we do not accept the changes occurring. Therefore, the right change can in fact be very rewarding for everyone.

However, when playing new games (products and services) in new playgrounds (markets), we must always beware! We must beware because; new rules are emerging all the time. We must understand those rules if we wish to follow them or try to change them (break them). Changing rules is necessary at times, but we should be aware of the outcome of those important rule-decisions (how they will affect our company). Therefore, knowing the rules of the game we are playing is necessary but, we must always be alert and sensitive to how business environment changes are impacting our game (products and services) and our playground (markets), today and tomorrow. Every organization should be on the lookout for new games (products and services) and new playgrounds (markets). They should do that because those opportunities might offer better conditions for realizing the larger plan.

The business environment can affect us, but it should not control us. Learning new games and discovering new playgrounds can help in managing the business environment. What this means is that, when we are comfortable with the rules of the game and the playground, we are 'surviving'. However, becoming 'all that we can be' means that we are constantly seeking out new games (products and services), and new playgrounds (markets). We are doing this because the environment is constantly changing, and we need to 'plan for change' (be on the lookout for new opportunities). That is a better alternative than letting change surprise us.

As one example of how the changing environment can impact strategy, the digitalization of businesses is a significant disrupter today. Therefore, every company should be considering the impact digitalization might have on their business. However, to understand the impact of digitalization, companies must ask a few critical questions;

1. Is our current business model viable (competitive on costs, engagement levels, control of operations etc.)?
2. Is our core business going to benefit from the change occurring, or do we need to transform

that business (new business, new competencies etc.)?
3. Is our operational model (capabilities) fit-for-purpose (supply chain, operations, channels etc.)?

Every organization must be continually evaluating opportunities and threats which may come because of the change occurring in their business environment. Furthermore, it is the job of management to continually evaluate their resource-allocation practices and priorities (resources must fit the emerging opportunities and threats). In addition, their capability (and cost) to change business practices must also be considered. Digitalization is just one of the many environmental forces which companies must consider today. Tomorrow there will be new forces emerging. Therefore, it is essential that management (and employees) develop a capability to gain insight into those emerging issues which may or may not impact their business. More importantly, everyone must learn to practice smart-thinking (and to share that thinking). Smart-thinking requires that the organization is ready to accept how unpredictable the environment has become, and how limited the organization is in dealing with the changes required. To become smart-learners, every organization should develop capabilities in the following skills;

- Assessing the environment and matching the findings with the appropriate strategy.
- Matching the strategy selected with the organizations capabilities (levels, functions etc.).
- Evaluating the selection and matching choices made (adjusting them accordingly).

- Selecting the right employees to manage the process (defining how this is to be done).
- Communicating choices made (integrated and understandable).
- Asking the right questions which fit with the company's context (seeking different views).
- Monitoring the business environment (what was overlooked or under-estimated).
- Focusing on the actions which have the greatest impact (overcoming resistance).

Employees and management are often afraid of change. Because of fear, they might even do everything they can to hold onto the past. People often become afraid because during an earlier time, they might have been able to ignore or prevent change from happening (their environment was a small village). However, that village is now becoming more global and we should not be afraid of this reality. Instead we should prepare ourselves to meet the challenges which the new environment will bring. Being prepared means that the organization has a plan, along with reasonable alternatives (just in case), for what might occur (due to the ever-changing environment). When you have a good plan; if one road is suddenly closed during the strategy journey, you can take another road and still reach the desired destination. Therefore, a good strategy must be supported by a contingency plan, (preparation to change), because the context every organization is operating in today is changing all the time.

The construction materials for every strategy (resources and the environment) change continuously. What this means is that strategies are alive, and that everyone must accept this fact (tomorrow will be different from today, and the necessary strategy will be different also). Unfortunately, most employees and companies dream of a life that has stopped and does not change. However, when an organization refuses to learn new games (products and services) and to play in new playgrounds (markets), they will also stop. The results of stopping will not be good for anybody (the world of tomorrow will not accept the world of yesterday). This simple fact means that employees and organizations must be continually making progress (positive change). To achieve that progress however, requires that they are constantly aware of what's going on around them (watching the radar screen). Furthermore, they should always be open to new opportunities, while remaining aware of the threats those opportunities might bring. Being prepared and open to change is a better alternative to being afraid of what might happen! This is true because; change can be profitable, while not changing can be deadly.

## CASE: DELIBERATE VS. EMERGENT STRATEGIES

*Professor Michael Porter (Harvard Business School) is the father of deliberate strategy analysis. Planning plays a central role in his strategy paradigm. In that paradigm, companies can have influence over the environments they find themselves in (Five Forces Analysis). However, some would argue that planning in an environment which exhibits continuous (discontinuous) change isn't useful. In fact, the days of 5 year, or even 2-year plans, are long gone. Today, companies must be much more agile and capable of strategic flexibility (Professor Henry Mintzberg on emergent strategy). Furthermore, the current market conditions make it harder and harder to carry out an effective industry analysis.*

*Macy's (US retailer) recognized already in the early 2000's that consumers were going online. The challenge for Macy's was that they had made a big commitment to their traditional store format (brick-and-mortar). However, Macy's also accepted that in such an uncertain environment it was not a question 'if' e-commerce would disrupt the market, but rather 'when' that would happen? Therefore, the company started to build its own online platform, experiment, and learn. Over time Macy's created a strong capability in e-commerce. Today web-based revenue is +$3 billion, more than 11% of the company's total sales, and growing at +40%.*

# CRITICAL QUESTIONS

1. Is there awareness (by everyone) of what's going on (define, describe and explain the change occurring in the game, the playground etc.)?
2. Do you (everyone) understand how change is impacting your business operations (and strategy)?
3. Have you defined, described and explained the benefits of changing behavior (and demonstrated the benefits of doing so through your actions)?
4. Is **everyone** aware of the findings from the above questions?

## TASK 4: WHAT IS YOUR APPROACH TO STRATEGY?

The business environment does and can influence greatly a company's strategy. However, it is important to know how the environment can impact the strategy. By taking the BCG Strategy Palette Survey you can determine the gaps which exist between your intended and actual strategic practices.

LINK: Strategy Palette Assessment
https://goo.gl/1RjoF3

Note: If you don't register at end of survey you will still see the results.

# SUMMARY

The managerial and employee communication challenges which need to be addressed.

### ENVIRONMENT

| MANAGEMENT | EMPLOYEES |
|---|---|
| ☑ Adjusting and adapting to conditions? | Recognize level of control vs dependency? ☒ |
| ◯ Following and influencing the rules? | Understand the game and playground? ◯ |
| ◯ Opportunity scanning and assessment? | Level of comfort, and fear (surprises)? ◯ |
| ◯ Building-in adaptability and flexibility? | Appreciate the benefits of change? ◯ |

## SOURCES:

- Scanlan, J. (2016). How Digital is Changing Strategy. McKinsey and Company
- Knowles, K. S. Holland, V. Melian, and F. Miller (2013). Organization Acceleration. Deloitte Development LLC
- Simester, Douglas (2016). The Lost Art of Thinking in Large Organizations. MIT Sloan Management Review
- Reeves, M. K. Haanaes, and J. Sinha. Your Strategy Needs A Strategy. Harvard Business Review Press

- Toner, Martin, N. Ohja, P. de Paepe, and M. de Mlo (2015): A Strategy for Thriving in Uncertainty. Bain and Co. Insights

# Profit

*'Profit helps us survive, and move beyond survival'*

The factors which can determine the quality of a company include;

- Profitability (obtaining higher margins).
- Low levels of debt (efficient cash management).
- Capable management (high return on invested capital/capital allocation).
- Business activities which are somewhat stable (a sustainable business model).

Profit is the best part of every successful strategy. This is true because profit tells us that the strategy we followed was the right one! Profit also tells us that we are moving in the right direction. Profit also allows us to invest more for the future. If we make the right investments for the future, we can almost guarantee that our profits in the future will also grow. Profit means that an organization can become more independent, comfortable, secure, and move beyond survival. In fact, profit is the paycheck for everyone's hard work.

High levels of trust have been linked with achieving high profits. Research by the Great Places to Work Institute for example, has shown that companies with high levels of trust between management and employees have outperformed the S&P 500 by a factor of 3X in the past fifteen years. However, there are other important metrics for measuring success (in addition to profit), which have an impact on every organization. Some of those metrics include;

- **Measures of Now**: Growth, return of capital, return on assets, KPI's and others.
- **Employee Measures**: The level of effort (engagement) employee puts towards enhancing the organizations performance, reputation and interests.
- **Measures of Purpose**: Culture, Mission, and Vision.

Selecting the right measure for success is important for every organization. However, to achieve success also requires the organization to have some unique strength. One important thing which makes a company stronger is when they compete against others. Competition is a good thing because; competition brings more profit (if it is fair). In fact, fair competition can be very good for business, because the strongest competitors are often the ones who profit the most.

Therefore, every organization should follow their roadmap to profit (and other critical metrics). However, when creating that roadmap, organizations can select from three broad competitive advantages (to maximize performance). High performing organizations tend to have all three of those advantages. Those three advantages include;

- **Consumer Advantage**: Differentiation of the companies offering compared to its competition.
- **Production Advantage**: Cost leadership over its competitors.
- **Economies of Scale**: Capability to increase output (although some businesses are not scale sensitive).

The research has shown that there are three additional factors which can also impact a company's performance over time;

1. Luck (can't be controlled).
2. Better-Before-Cheaper (never competing on price).
3. Revenue-Before-Cost (increasing sales, rather than cutting costs).

## Sustainable Profitability

According to Professor Stuart Harborne (Columbia University), many organizations are unable to explain why they are profitable, and how their profitability is linked to their strategy. Furthermore, often those companies' strategies have not considered the sustainability of their profitability.

The first step to understanding profitability, in relation to strategy, is to understand where profits come from. Sustainable profits in fact, come mostly from customer value creation. Furthermore, the level of sustainable profits achieved is also influenced by competitive conditions (how value-creation is divided between industry players, along with the price-setting strategies of those players). Competitive advantage is therefore an important element in determining profitability (and in strategy). If an advantage does not exist, then the organization must rely solely on marketing tactics or operational efficiency, if they wish to create more customer value.

As a share of total income, corporate profits today (USA) are at a level of +13.5% to +14% (Pre-1990 levels were +8.5%). Therefore, in recent times companies (based on S&P 500 analysis) have seen a huge increase in profits. Productivity gains (+5% to + 7%) and technological progress have played a minor role in that profit growth (although they do impact costs). The rapid growth in profitability recently has also not been due to growing market demand (current growth rates are +2% to +3%, which is slightly behind the mean 25-year sale growth rate). In addition to those points, the gross profit margin level for companies (+-30%) has remained stagnant for the past 25 years.

However, operating profitability has seen a healthy level of growth since 2004 (+13.5% in 2014). Those operating profits have been increased by reducing the; sales, general and administrative expenses (SGA) in companies. Declining SGA in fact has made the largest contribution to the current rapid growth in profitability (rather than productivity gains or service economy growth etc.).

Another factor which has contributed to higher profitability levels has been low borrowing costs. The mean level of borrowing costs was 7% over the past 24 years. However, the latest figures indicate that interest rates today are below 4% (if not lower). What this means is that, if interest rates were to rise to the historical mean levels, overall corporate profitability would decline by -11%. Corporate tax rates have also had a positive impact on profitability recently. Corporate tax rates in fact have declined since 2007-2008 (+-40%), and currently stand at a level below 30%.

What the above review tells us is that; there are multiple factors which can impact a company's profitability. However; the major contributor to the recent increase in corporate profitability has been intensive cost-cutting, along with reductions in capital expenditures (managing SGA). These increased profits are in fact a result of the shortening time-horizons which management are using in their decision making (to maximize short-term shareholder value). This short-termism is also impacting negatively corporate life-spans (currently around 15 years for S&P 500 companies), along with shortening the tenure of CEO's (from 10 years to 6 years today).

Improving profitability by cutting SGA expenses and postponing capital investments can and does have serious implications for sustainable profitability (and competitiveness) in the long-term for every business. Beware of this dangerous short-term trick!

## CALCULATING PERFORMANCE

There are many financial metrics for measuring performance. However, every metric has its pro's and con's. The challenge is to determine which financial metrics are best suited to your individual strategy! It is also important to remember that there are non-financial metrics (Employee Measures and Measures of Purpose). Some of the most critical financial metrics to consider include;

- **Gross Profit**: The difference between sales and cost of goods sold (including depreciation).
- **Gross Profit Margin**: Gross profit divided by sales (gross profit/sales).
- **Operating Profit**: Gross profit minus SGA (SGA sales, general, and administrative expenses).
- **Operating Profitability**: Operating profit divided by sales.
- **Net Profit Margin**: After-tax net profit divided by sales.
- **Return on Equity (ROE)**: Net income divided by shareholder equity (investment efficiency).
- **Return on Assets (ROA)**: Earnings divided by assets.
- **Return on Invested Capital (ROIC)**: Net operating profit (after tax) divided by invested capital (capital employed).
- **Return on Incremental Invested Capital (ROIIC)**: The relationship between incremental investment and incremental net operating profit.

## CASE: +800% Profit at Amazon

*In the second quarter of 2016, Amazon recorded a +800% increase in profits (compared to 2015's second quarter). Was that profit an indication of a change in the strategy for Amazon?*

*Previously, Amazon had re-invested all its profits back into building the business empire (staying '100 steps ahead of the competition'). Those investments included; building new fulfillment centers and expanding hardware activities (smartphones etc.). Many of those investments are now paying off handsomely (cloud platform etc.). In fact, Amazon is profitable in almost all their activities however, in the past that profit ('every last penny') was re-invested back into the business!*

*Does Amazon need to return to re-investing all profits to stay '100 steps ahead of the competition' in the future?*

# CRITICAL QUESTIONS

1. How does your company make and measure profit today?
2. Do you have a roadmap for sustainable profits; have you defined the metrics, describe the necessary actions, communicate those actions, and explained the anticipated outcomes?
3. Have you made a commitment to strengthen your resources (where, how and why are the profits used)?
4. Is **everyone** aware of the findings from the above questions?

# SUMMARY

**The managerial and employee communication challenges which need to be addressed.**

## PROFIT

| MANAGEMENT | EMPLOYEES |
|---|---|
| ✓ Defining the desirable outcomes? | ✗ I/we understand individual contributions? |
| ○ Processes for making and measuring profit? | ○ How I/we contribute to profit creation? |
| ○ Creating a profit (cost) roadmap? | ○ Level of effort required, and limitations? |
| ○ Supporting sustainable profitability? | ○ What is the reward for me & others? |

## SOURCES:

- Financial Performance: Trust Fuels Business Outcomes (2016). Great Places to Work
- Atkins. Andy, (2014). Building Workplace Trust: Trends and High Performance. Interaction Associates
- Hagel, John, J. Seeley Brown, T. Samoylova (2013). Success or Struggle-ROA As a True Measure of Business Performance. Deloitte University Press
- Connecting the Dots-How Purpose Can Join Up Your Business (2016). PwC Global
- Harborne. Stuart (2016) The Profitability Test: Does Your Strategy Make Sense? The MIT Press
- Harmika. Baijnath (2014). Why Jeremy Grantham is Right About Corporate Profit Margins. Advisor Perspectives
- Rotonti. John (2016). Interview with Michael Mauboussin (Columbia University). The Motley Fool
- Mauboussin. Michael, and Dan Callahan (2014). Capital Allocation: Evidence, Analytical Methods, and Assessment Guidance. Credit Suisse
- Michael. Raynor and M. Ahmed (2013). Three Rules: How Exceptional Companies Think. Deloitte Review

# Competition
### *'Is competition a good or bad thing?*

Life is a competition (worms compete, birds compete, and people compete). In fact, most people find competition to be quite natural, even though we may find ourselves fighting every day. However, it is important to remember that success in business is made up of many battles. Concentrating on the battle we are fighting today is important but keeping in mind the big picture is even more important. Therefore, every company should have a grand strategy for fighting the competition (which may involve many small battles).

It also helps to have rules for engagement during competition. This helps because nobody wants to get killed on the battlefield, and those rules make it possible for us to compete on a fair basis. Furthermore, companies should be able to decide how competitive they want to be (this does not mean that you get a free ride). Some of the battles we fight will have an upside and some a downside. However, if we want to fight harder it's acceptable, and if we don't, that is also acceptable (because trying harder might also fail). Having an understandable strategy helps everyone know how competitive they wish to be, and which battles they must fight. When making decisions on these important competitive actions, management must always keep in mind the game (product and services), playground (market), available resources, environment, and the rewards they seek (profits). Furthermore, a company's strategy must be built upon unique skills and capabilities.

The best way to be successful in competition is by making the right choices (game, playing field etc.) which best fit the resources a company bring to the table. Furthermore, if a company is weak in resources, they should use their profits to strengthen themselves. However, remember that competition is not only about making war. Competition can also encourage a company discover better quality, better prices, better profits, and a better life for everyone. Also, competition should not be only about winners and losers. The goal in fact should be to create more winners. This is possible because, successful competition helps to create a bigger group of winners.

Another important principle to remember regarding competition is that; the more a company wins, the more likely it is that they will win in the future. Winning once feels good, but winning most of the time feels great. However, companies who are not accustomed to winning are less likely to win in the future. This principle is important to remember because;

> ***When we win, we feel better about ourselves, and begin to understand that winning makes us a winner again... and again!***

Companies don't need to win 100% of the time, although occasional wins are necessary for survival. A good strategy helps a company to survive; a great strategy brings wins more and more often. Fair competition should of course be the source of a company's success. This is because; fair competition makes a company stronger and improves the likelihood of future profits. However, please keep in mind that competition is more about direction than a bad attitude (always trying to beat everyone). When a company takes the right direction (based on the right strategy), they may not even need to have a big fight. Therefore, having a bad attitude is not necessary because competition should be natural, beneficial, and something a company does every day... it's their job.

You might be wondering by now; why have we not taken a deep-dive into the traditional strategy tools which companies have relied on for decades (BCG matrix, 5-Forces, Generic Strategies, Sustainable Competitive Advantage etc.). Those traditional strategy tools in fact are becoming increasingly obsolete because of the rapidly changing environment companies are faced with today.

Professor Rita McGrath (Columbia Business School) in her research has demonstrated that few companies have the capability to obtain sustainable above-average returns (despite all the tools available to help them). Of the 4,793 companies studied by Prof. McGrath, only 10 of those companies were in fact able to achieve a +5% annual net income growth over a period of 10 years. Those companies who achieved a superior net income growth over that time (the 1% Outlier Club) had deployed unique strategies. Prof. McGrath says that outliers use exploratory strategies, rather than traditional strategy models (sustainable advantage, competitive advantage etc.). Moreover, this flip in strategy/income performance is occurring because;

- Sustainable competitive advantage has become less and less obtainable.
- Industry and market barriers to entry are being eroded.
- More agile organizational forms are emerging (stability is dangerous).
- Hierarchical organizations and information-intensive organizations are facing increased pressure to transform themselves (information efficiency is becoming a critical performance metric).
- Flexibility is being favored over optimization.
- Industry boundaries are continuously being eroded (resources have become the main advantage, not industry-specific capabilities).
- Continuous re-configuration is now an essential capability, along with learning to dis-engage from industries (leaving industry in an organized way, rather than dying a slow death).
- Resource allocation, decision making, and the pace of change are accelerating (agile capabilities are needed).

- Powerful information system-capability has become a differentiator.
- Innovation capability is becoming an essential and continuous process.
- Leadership today is less about operational effectiveness and more about seeking out new information and continuous experimentation (risk taking).

Therefore, the game (products and services), the rules of the game, the playing field (markets), and the players are changing. This means that the competitors we will face tomorrow are going to be different than today. Moreover, the changes occurring will also make it harder for companies to compete successfully in the future. Therefore, every company must be willing to learn new ways to compete (games and playgrounds). This is necessary because; the world is becoming more global every day, and we must all wake up to the changes which that globalization brings.

## CRITICAL QUESTIONS

1. Have you decided how competitive you wish to be (and are)?
2. Have you defined, described and explained how the strategy supports that competitiveness?
3. Have you created systems to; celebrate victories, learn from failures and change attitudes?
4. Is **everyone** aware of the findings from the above questions?

# SUMMARY

**The managerial and employee communication challenges which need to be addressed.**

## COMPETITION

| | MANAGEMENT | | EMPLOYEES | |
|---|---|---|---|---|
| ✓ | Create competitive posture and capability? | | What is my/our unique contribution (skill)? | ✗ |
| ○ | Define rules of engagement (competitiveness)? | | What are the priorities (quality...)? | ○ |
| ○ | Exploring alternatives? | | What changes are needed (experimenting)? | ○ |
| ○ | Celebrating? | | How I/we are improving and benefiting? | ○ |

## SOURCES:

- Schwab, Klaus. And X. Sala-I-Martin (2016): The Global Competitiveness Report 2016/2017. World Economic Forum
- McGrath, Rita Gunter (2013). The End of Competitive Advantage. Harvard Business Review

# Globalization

*'Will the game and the playground for your company remain the same?'*

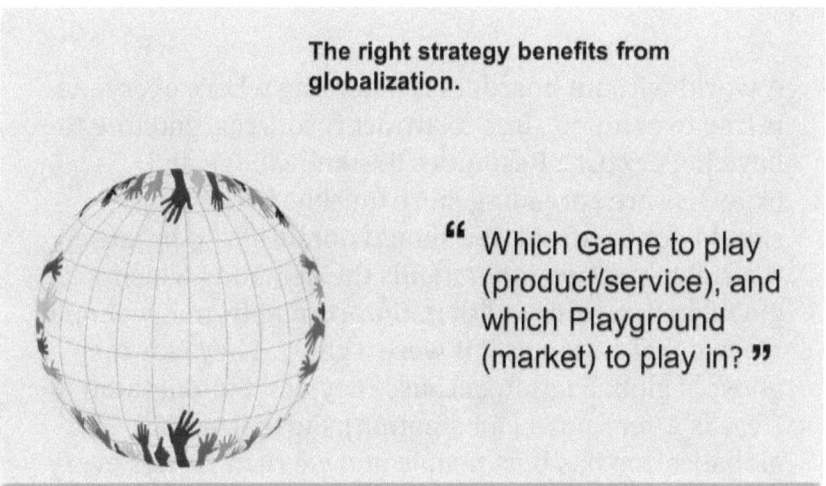

The right strategy benefits from globalization.

" Which Game to play (product/service), and which Playground (market) to play in? "

Globalization means that new games and playing fields are emerging all the time. Because of this trend, some competitors will get stronger and others will get weaker. Furthermore, the new players may have different resources, and unique home-environments which give them advantages. However, first we must accept the fact that environments are changing, and competition is becoming more global.

In fact, companies throughout the world are always looking for new markets and new sources of profit. With the right strategy, those companies will survive and even prosper. If your company has the right strategy, you can also prosper and profit. With that profit you can then invest more for the future.

Globalization will be a serious threat if you are not prepared to answer its challenges.

## *How many of the companies you competed with in the past have disappeared or changed their game?*

A world without boarders is emerging where everyone is free to compete, free to attract resources, and free to have lower costs. Resources like knowledge and expertise are spreading more quickly. However, we should not be afraid. We should not be afraid because, the right strategy understands the demands which globalization brings with it. Unfortunately, many people view globalization as if it were a ghost. They fear the ghost of globalization because they don't understand it (fear is a very powerful emotion). Furthermore, globalization has hurt people and we read stories every day in the news which remind us of that reality. However, we should all remember that globalization is just another form of competition, and globalization reminds us that we must continuously improve our competitiveness.

Being competitive means that we learn to play new games (products and services), and to play in new playgrounds (markets). It is also essential that we know and understand our new enemies. Furthermore, we should remember that a good enemy is better than a lazy friend. In addition to these points, we should never stop what we are doing properly, just because we have encountered a bigger challenge. Giving up is not an option if we are capable of learning new ways of doing business, and our resources can adapt to meet whatever globalization might bring.

McKinsey and Company have identified the six critical globalization dimensions which can impact every company;

- **Global Footprint**: The traditional approach favored by companies is to replicate (duplicate) existing structures in foreign markets. However, the opportunity to capture efficiency and scale by using alternative structures is growing (are you experimenting with new structures?).
- **Localization vs. Standardization**: Individual market needs, and regulations must always be considered (how does standardized, or localized impact your value proposition?).
- **Operational Agility**: More than 2/3 of global manufacturing occurs close to demand. However, the emergence of digital technologies and their impact on supply chain management must be re-evaluated (do you have the necessary level of agility).
- **Digital Platforms**: Advanced digital capabilities are becoming a new source of competitive advantage (do you have or are you developing those capabilities?)
- **Global Competition**: Lean, agile and aggressive competitors are emerging who also have cost advantages. The Topple-Rate (rate at which companies lose their leading market position) has increased +40% in recent time (what are your chances of being toppled, and why?).
- **Risk Management**: Diversified supply chains reduce risks (what is your supply-chain risk exposure?). One industry facing high risks is the

pharmaceutical industry (currently over-reliant on single-site supplies).

Please remember that profit was the happiest part of a good strategy. Therefore, a company should be more than happy to invest their profits to become stronger for tomorrow's global marketplace. Part of the plan for tomorrow should also consider growing your business.

## CRITICAL QUESTIONS

1. What is your company's attitude to globalization (understanding, fear, ignorance, etc.)?
2. Is your strategy addressing the challenges globalization brings with it (why, how)?
3. How will new playgrounds (markets) and new games (products and services) affect your company (positive effects, negative effects, and necessary actions)?
4. Is **everyone** aware of the findings from the above questions?

# SUMMARY

The managerial and employee communication challenges which need to be addressed.

## GLOBALIZATION

| MANAGEMENT | EMPLOYEES |
|---|---|
| ✓ I.D. new markets and sources of profit? | ✗ Why is globalization good/bad for me/us? |
| ○ Monitor competitor capabilities? | ○ What are our rules for competing? |
| ○ Configure and coordinating value? | ○ What skills I/we need to strengthen (why)? |
| ○ Architect the change management process? | ○ What are the risks of refusing to change? |

*Let's Talk*

## SOURCES:

- Globalization and New Strategies for Growth: The World is Bumpy (2011). Ernst and Young
- Manyika. J. et all (2016). Digital Globalization- The New Era of Global Flows. McKinsey and Company

# Growth
*"Moderation"*

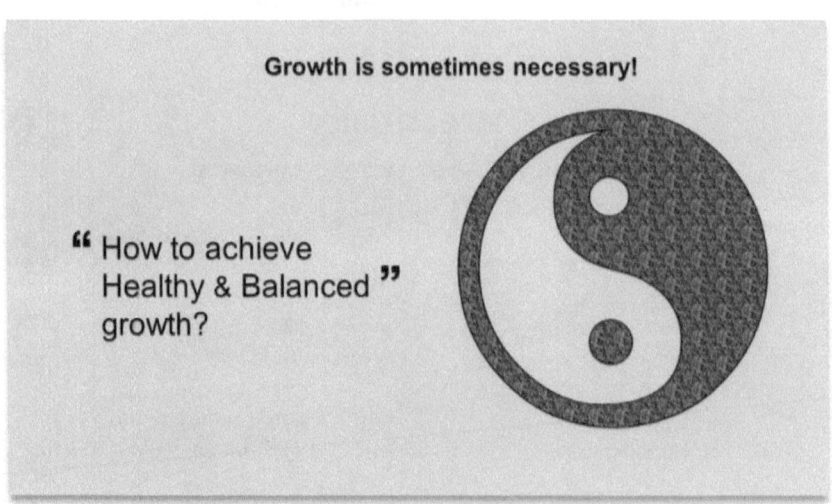

Growth can help a company become 'all that they can be'. However, balanced growth is necessary. What this means is that any growth should be balanced to serve the companies purpose. One of the most important things to remember about growth is the speed at which growth occurs. Speed is important because, too fast is bad and too slow can also be bad. Therefore, companies need to manage (moderate) their growth.

It does not always make sense to grow bigger without achieving some benefits. Those benefits might include profits to invest for the future. Remember though, growth 'for the sake of growth', is like a dog chasing its tail. In other words, growth must always bring with it advantages and benefits. Growth is a decision, and for those who have a need to grow it can be a good decision. However, even in those cases, growth should be done in the right way; with a plan and designed to avoid mistakes. In addition to having a growth plan, the right attitude and willpower is necessary. However, having a plan, the right attitude and willpower, are still not enough. Successful growth also depends on the business environment, competition, resources and more. These factors need to be considered because, uncontrolled growth can bring with it many problems (just ask any farmer about that).

The strains (and complexity) which accompany growth must also be considered. One must also consider how growth will impact existing and future organizational processes. If the impact is found to be significant, then the necessary capabilities must be put in-place to deal with those growing pains, which are part and parcel of a growth strategy. Companies should also account for the following;

- Are the existing organizational structures optimized for the 'old way' of doing business? Changing existing structures can take years to implement successfully (or be proven to work).
- Are the current business processes scaleable? Stress-tests may be needed to determine if those processes can handle future demands (growth).
- Are the company's human resource, structures and tasks-completion capabilities ready? This is important to assess because, complexity grows as the organization grows, and more agile organizational capabilities might be needed to deal with that increasing complexity.

Making decisions is also an important part of any strategy, and the need for growth is one important decision. If the answer to 'should we grow' is yes, then there must be a clear purpose for that decision (supports business development, need to acquire new skills, etc.). Furthermore, the desired level of growth must be profitable. It must be profitable because; when we profit, everyone can satisfy their needs, make their lives easier and invest for the future. Please remember though; growth is not always necessary. However, if growth is the goal of the company's strategy it must be planned well. Smart-planning should **involve as many employees as possible in the process.**

## CASE: THE TORTOISE AND THE HARE

*Groupon.com wanted to grow big, fast and furiously. Steals.com decided instead to grow steady, and it's working.*

*Unlike Groupon, Steals does not overwhelm customers with emails or special deals continuously. Instead they offer just two deals a day (in stock and with same day shipping). That decision has resulted in Steals becoming profitable earlier, and the brand exposure suppliers get is superior to anything Groupon can offer (only two brand deals a day).*

*The hyper-growth model Groupon deployed worked for them however, the Tortoise 'slow growth model' used by Steals.com works for them also. If you don't want to live the life of a Hare, slow is also a healthy alternative.*

## CRITICAL QUESTIONS

1. How does growth support you company's strategy (why)?
2. How does growth contribute to higher levels of profitability?
3. How does growth enhance the company's value proposition, benefits to customers, competitiveness, and capabilities (employee and skills development etc.)?
4. Is **everyone** aware of the findings from the above questions?

# SUMMARY

**The managerial and employee communication challenges which need to be addressed.**

## GROWTH

| MANAGEMENT | EMPLOYEES |
|---|---|
| ✓ Defining healthy and balanced growth levels? | How does growth serve my/our purpose? ✗ |
| ○ Putting in place a growth plan? | Why should I/we put in the effort? ○ |
| ○ Assessing impact on organization (complexity)? | Why (how) are changes being made? ○ |
| ○ Implementing agile processes? | Do I/we have, or can acquire, necessary skills? ○ |

## SOURCES:

> Dewhurst. Martin, S. Heywood, K. Rieckhoff (2011). Preparing Your Organization for Growth. McKinsey Quarterly

# Planning

*"Smart-Planning, Makes Perfect"*

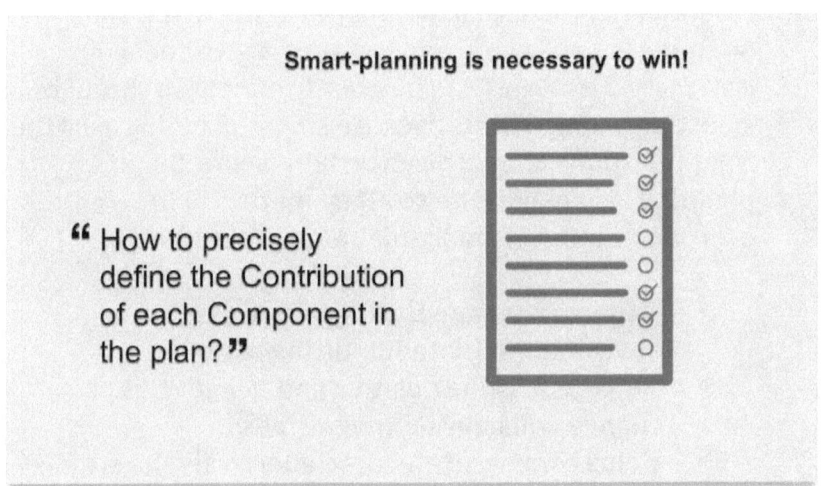

Planning is often considered to be a complicated process. However, what a plan simply means is that; the company must think about what to do, why they are doing it, and how to do it. Planning is not strategy, but it is an important part of the strategy process. Companies are planning all the time (short-term and long term). Short-term plans are often more tactical and long-term plans are more strategic. In today's fast changing business environment, planning is in fact becoming more and more important. However, we should remember that planning is not only about staring into a crystal ball, in the hope of seeing the future. Planning should also involve; doing, learning and adjusting. Furthermore, planning should be personal, customized, involve experimentation, and allow companies to test new ideas (safely). This form of planning we refer to as smart-planning.

Because the environment is changing rapidly, it is essential to practice smart-planning. However, smart-planning is hard work, and requires a great deal of creativity. Strategies can be greatly enhanced through smart-planning. This is because smart-planning asks the right questions about the uncertain future. Smart-planning also makes the strategy more real in everyone's mind. A smart-planning process;

- Helps to navigate the foggy business environment (without hitting rocks).
- Helps assess the positive and negative impact change will have on the business.
- Helps communicate more effectively the strategy to all employees.
- Helps manage resources.
- Help bring order to everyday routines.

Strategy communicates to employees and management where they are going, but smart-planning helps everyone pull in the same direction. When everyone pulls in the same direction, they will more likely get safely to where they are going. Smart-planning also opens employees' minds and frees them to discover new ways of doing old things. Therefore, smart-planning is a way to discover new habits and change old habits. What this means is that; the real value from smart-planning is to; see the environment in a new way, and by doing so recognize new opportunities. However, to plan well a company must also have the essential and relevant information (facts).

A smart planning process should involve as many employees as possible, who can openly share their ideas and their dreams. In a smart-planning process, employees need not be afraid to let others know what they think. This is important because a diversity of ideas might in fact help everyone learn, profit from that learning and grow (avoid confirmation bias). The reward of smart-planning is that employees will be more likely to give 110% to the plan and the strategy.

Research by Bain and Co. has shown than fewer than 1 in 3 executives feel that their strategy planning process offers 'concrete guidance for management and the front line'. However, companies that have produced great strategies view the planning process as a critical capability and are always trying to make that planning process world-class. The message here is that the planning process can be very beneficial, but it should be done in a smart way. Smart-planning requires some of the following elements;

- The planning must be crafted independently from operational budgeting (just this action can improve strategies by +40% according to Bain and Co.).
- The planning must consider the voice of the customer, along with the company's front-line personnel.
- The plan must allocate resources based on strategic priorities, growth opportunities and re-deploying resources when needed (an un-democratic decision-making process).
- The planning must follow a continuous (24/7/365), issues-based, and strategic agenda (when circumstances change rapidly in the

business environment, the planning process also needs to change).
- The planning must be simplified and follow zero-based planning principles (beginning with a blank piece of paper).

Strategic planning is a process during which a company can determine what their business should become in the future, and how to achieve that goal. During the strategic planning process management must assess the potential for their business, and define the specific activities needed to achieve that potential. Therefore, strategic planning must address the most critical questions that may impact the company (resource commitment etc.). The steps taken during the typical smart-planning process should include;

- Defining the organizations mission, vision and values.
- Investigating potential business opportunities.
- Identifying and monitoring emerging threats and opportunities.
- Identifying, defining and understanding the different customer segments and priority target segments.
- Measuring the company's strengths and weakness in relation to competitors.
- Determining make vs. buy decisions (outsourcing, off-shoring etc.).
- Evaluating different strategic alternatives.
- Engineering an effective business model which delivers the required profits and differentiates the company from others.

- Defining and articulating the business objectives and measures of performance – key performance indicators (KPI's etc.).
- Constructing programs, guidelines, policies and plans to support strategy implementation.
- Designing organizational structures which support the objectives (decision processes, information systems, human resource development etc.).
- Allocating resources to different business areas and for the development of critical capabilities.
- Identifying, measuring, monitoring and evaluating the risks, along with preparing contingency plans to deal with those risks.
- Measuring, monitoring, and holding accountable management for the performance levels achieved (not achieved).

Strategic planning is half the battle because the plan tells everyone what direction they should be moving in. However, teamwork is the other half of the battle. Teamwork is important to planning because, when effective teamwork is successful, everyone will be pulling in the exact same direction. When everyone pulls at the same time, and in the same direction, the strategy comes to life!

## CASE: A BAD STRATEGY, IS BAD FOR BUSINESS?

*According to Professor Richard Rumelt (UCLA), 'bad strategy covers up its failure to guide by embracing the language of broad goals, ambitions, vision, and values (let's win). Companies with bad strategies have not even defined the problems they are facing. Creating a template for the; Vision, Mission, Values, Purpose, and Strategies is also a recipe for failure.' Good strategies, on the other hand, help organizations navigate through difficult times, respond to challenges, and overcome obstacles during the journey.*

*Digital Equipment Corporation (DEC) was the leader of the minicomputer revolution in 1970's. DEC in 1992 however, was declining rapidly. The CEO at that time (Ken Olsen) asked top management for their views on what to do (based on three alternatives). The challenge for the management team was to decide which one alternative to go with. However; the management team could not agree on just one of the alternatives (The Condorcet's paradox). The result was that management made a compromise (the fluffy' choice). That choice was not a strategy; it was a politically correct choice which was made based on a consensus, rather than taking a position!*

*In 1998, DEC was acquired by Compaq (who was later acquired by Hewlett Packard in 2001).*

# CRITICAL QUESTIONS

1. Do your plans/planning process consider the ideas and dreams of everyone (if not, what action is needed)?
2. Are the right employees (who), and enough employees, involved in the planning process?
3. How does the planning process engage with everyone (listening, transparency, communication and sharing)?
4. Is **everyone** aware of the findings from the above questions?

# SUMMARY

**The managerial and employee communication challenges which need to be addressed.**

## PLANNING

| MANAGEMENT | EMPLOYEES |
|---|---|
| ✓ Using smart planning (plan, do, learn, adjust)? | ✗ How predictable or uncertain is the future? |
| ○ Ensuring everyone is moving in same direction? | ○ What does the future mean for me/us? |
| ○ Reporting & sharing relevant information (facts)? | ○ Required level of risks vs commitment? |
| ○ Monitoring teamwork and engagement effectiveness? | ○ What is my/our contribution and why? |

**SOURCES:**

- Mark Judah, D. O'Keeffe, D. Zehner (2016). Strategic Planning That Produces Real Strategy
- Richard Rumelt (2011). The Perils of Bad Strategy. McKinsey Quarterly

# Making Strategy Happen!

*Every person has a desire to accomplish some purpose therefore; every employee can add value to strategy.*

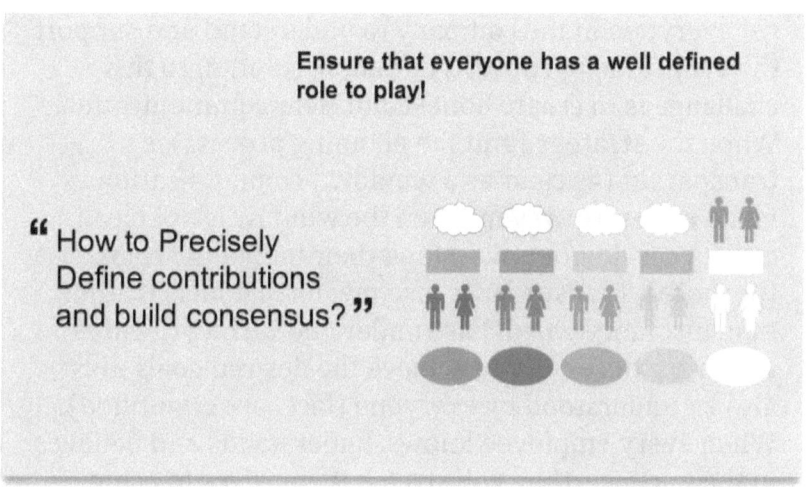

People need to complete things, and the things they complete are more rewarding, if they are good at them. Purpose is essential to achieving a successful strategy. However, that purpose must be made very clear and be easily understood by everyone. A company's purpose is in fact important to every employee's individual purpose. However, making this connection is not easy and can encounter many roadblocks. Most of those roadblocks can be removed if we are honest with one another. Wanting to win and having the ability to win is not in fact the biggest roadblock. One of the biggest roadblocks is the lack of effective communication between management and employees. This communication gap is a major roadblock because; employees will not understand the companies' purpose (goal). If all employees do not understand, and can't relate to the companies' purpose, how can we expect them to stretch themselves in support of that purpose?

Therefore, the real challenge for management is; how to get everyone in the company to understand and support the very same purpose? The simple solution to this challenge is to create honest and clear communication. When the strategy (and the planning process) is transparent (as clear as a window,) communication is made easier. However, when the window is not clean, employees do not understand their individual roles (purpose). Transparency also means that facts (rather than just fancy words) are understood. The priorities which are necessary to achieve the desired goals must also be understood by everyone (facts are quantified). When every employee knows, understands and believes in the purpose, they will stretch themselves to achieve that purpose.

Strategy communication should not be a one-way street (a monologue) and must flow in many directions. In addition, employees must be listened to and heard. Everyone must also hear what must be said, and honest communication is the only way to achieve that. Honesty means that employees can freely discuss all matters connected to the strategy (the good, the bad and the ugly). Open and honest communication also helps employees to stretch themselves in a disciplined manner (the safest limit of their skills). A great strategy in fact, pulls every individual with it (in a disciplined manner). This is a good thing because; stretching allows employees to better understand their purpose, and to realize that they have some control over that purpose (and amount of individual effort). However, a common purpose also involves relationships and roles with others (we are never alone). This doesn't mean that individuals are not unique however; the company purpose can tie individuals together (in a team, with a common goal and through a common understanding of the strategy).

Discipline is required to control the level of stretch experienced by every employee. Discipline is important because; stretching without discipline is like stretching an elastic band too far (it may break). Therefore, management control must be exercised in the whole organization. This means that the stretching of every employee should be optimized, to achieve the best results. However, a challenge for management is;

***How to get the commitment and willingness to stretch (increased effort) from all employees?***

According to Professor Quy Huy (INSEAD), there are five reasons why organizations fail to effectively execute strategies. The number one reason is that organizations have not established a sense of urgency and commitment (stretch), in order to achieve a common goal. This lack of urgency and commitment occurs because;

- Mistrust and limited sharing of information is practiced.
- Leadership does not demonstrate their personal commitment and willingness to change.
- There is a lack of emotional engagement (more talk than action), and leaders have failed to engage everyone in the journey.

- There is a lack of risk taking, and innovative thinking processes.
- There is a strong belief in the status quo (the existing way is the best way), and that other ways require too much effort and risk.

Deciding on, and managing how much stretch is necessary, requires leaders to make important value judgements. Judgement in fact is a discipline which the leadership of every organization must always cultivate. This is because, good judgement when combined with clear priorities, can be extremely effective when planning and executing a strategy. When leaders can identify and define clear and understandable priorities that are based on good judgement, followers will emerge. However, to achieve the necessary levels of stretch (effort), leaders must continually remind employees of the important role they are all playing in the strategy. Only by doing this, can the organization stretch everyone, and by doing so achieve the desired results.

## CRITICAL QUESTIONS

- Is the company's purpose understandable, practiced and adding value for customers?
- Have the company's priorities and goals been described in ways that get employees' attention and excites them?
- Have management defined, described and explained what is needed/expected (from every employee), in order to successfully achieve the defined purpose, priorities and goals?
- Is everyone aware of the findings from the above questions?

# SUMMARY

**The managerial and employee communication challenges which need to be addressed.**

### MAKING IT HAPPEN

| MANAGEMENT | EMPLOYEES |
|---|---|
| ✓ Crafting a compelling and clear purpose? | ✗ How the strategy fits my/our purpose? |
| ○ Defining & clarifying goals and expectations? | ○ What is expected of me/us and why? |
| ○ Focusing on customer orientation? | ○ How the customer benefits from me/us? |
| ○ Supporting teamwork and engagement? | ○ What is my/our contribution and why? |

# SOURCES:

- Huy, Quy, (2016). Five Reasons Most Companies Fail at Strategy Execution. INSEAD Knowledge

# Leadership
*"Doing the right things"*

**Leaders guide employees towards the final destination!**

> Gaining TRUST (belief) for; a uncertain strategy, which may deliver everyone safely to the destination?

When thinking about strategy, the role of leadership is vital to understand. That leadership role is mostly about communication. Effective communication means that everyone, must always know where they are going, why they are going there, and how they are getting there! Effective communication informs people of that message. Effective communication also reminds employees of the desired goals, common values, and the individual actions needed to accomplish the desired goals. Furthermore, effective communication keeps everyone excited.

The company's strategy is the lighthouse, which guides everyone safely towards meeting individual and organizational goals. Therefore, every day, and for every action, management and employees need to be guided. Communication (the light in the lighthouse), must be crystal clear. Furthermore, the right behavior should be demonstrated, recognized and rewarded. The light from the lighthouse makes employees aware of; why they are doing what they are doing. The light (communication), also gets employees excited, gets their attention, motivates them, and helps them satisfy their personal motives. However, communication also must reflect the; wants, needs, goals and values of the whole organization. More importantly, employees should trust the communication. Employees must trust the strategy communication because;

***Trust is the emotional glue that binds everyone to the strategy. Without trust, the light will no longer shine in the lighthouse.***

Finally, one of the most crucial roles for leadership is to continually remind employees that every participant in the strategy process is important. Leadership is in fact all about making all employees feel important. This is essential because; employees do want to make a genuine contribution, and great leadership allows employees to do just that! By doing so, management can help create a supportive community (a family). However, an effective community also means that individual and community goals must be aligned and driven by a common purpose. Common purpose can only be realized if everyone is following the same light, from the same lighthouse, and the lighthouse keeper (leaders), are reminding employees of this every single day.

Trust always comes into the equation. Trust enters the equation because; leaders are always trying to get ordinary people to achieve awesome results. However, those results will only be realized after trust has been established (safe environment). Once trust has been established, personal security is enhanced, and only then can the actions of every individual employee live in harmony with the companies' purpose. However, to achieve the necessary levels of trust, leaders must;

- Continually help everyone move forward (remove barriers).
- Communicate a collective understanding of the strategy.
- Make the objectives and goals crystal clear, and understandable.
- Behave in ways that demonstrate good example.
- Actively commit themselves to the strategy.

Great strategic leadership is only achieved when; everyone knows where they are going, why they are going there, how they are going there, and what's different about how they're getting there. Great leaders can support this understanding because they are; very familiar with the roadmap and can describe everyone's role (throughout the journey), in ways which everyone can understand. The reward for great leadership will be that; employees have faith in their leaders and make more effort. This will only occur when great leaders;

- Respect every employee.
- Listen to employee dreams.
- Appreciate employee concerns.
- Believe that everyone makes an important contribution to the strategy.
- Believe that all employees have an important role to play.

Great leaders help others achieve their goals, and in the process of doing so, employees and the company can begin the journey of achieving 'all that they can be'. The greatest reward for leadership is more positive energy and effort from everyone in the organization (towards making the strategy a success).

## CRITICAL QUESTIONS

- How does/should leadership behave (commitment, example etc.)?
- How does/should leadership inform, explain and remind everyone of the company's purpose (understandable)?
- How does/should leadership ensure the safety and good will of everyone (good judgement and levels of trust)?
- Is **everyone** aware of the findings from the above questions?

## TASK 5: HOW EFFECTIVE ARE YOU AS A LEADER?

Take just eight minutes of your time to assess your leadership capability (16 competencies), and compare the results with 45,000 leaders throughout the world (Zenger/Folkman).

LINK: Zenger Folkman Leadership Assessment
https://goo.gl/t6ZR3T

Note: Registration is required (professional results are delivered)

# SUMMARY

**The managerial and employee communication challenges which need to be addressed.**

## LEADERSHIP

| | MANAGEMENT | EMPLOYEES | |
|---|---|---|---|
| ✓ | Are we leading by example? | Is the system fair and equal? | ✗ |
| ○ | Are we competent, capable and supportive? | Can I/we trust in leaders? | ○ |
| ○ | Is our strategic messaging & communication understood? | How informed am I/we (bad & good facts)? | ○ |
| ○ | Have we considered and accounted for safety? | Do I know where I/we are going and why? | ○ |

# SOURCES:

> Shoemaker, P. S. Krupp and s. Howland (2013). Strategic Leadership-The Essential Skills. Harvard Business Review

# Strategy Tools

Since 1993, Bain and Company have been tracking the use of management tool usage and the trends in usage. Successful use of these tools is based on the proper selection of the right tool (strength and weakness), along with the capability to integrate tools (at the right time). In the table below the Top 10 Tools are listed, along with their level of usefulness (satisfaction) for management. However, when considering the use of these tools management must always consider; ease of implementation, effectiveness, strengths and weaknesses.

| TOOL | USAGE % | SATISFACTION |
| --- | --- | --- |
| CRM | 46% | 3.93 |
| Benchmarking | 44% | 3.80 |
| Employee Engagement | 44% | 3.75 |
| Strategic Planning | 44% | 3.93 |
| Outsourcing | 41% | 3.61 |
| Balanced Scorecard | 38% | 3.90 |
| Mission and Vision | 38% | 3.82 |
| Supply Chain Management | 36% | 3.85 |
| Change Management | 34% | 3.69 |
| Customer Segmentation | 30% | 3.96 |

Source: Bain and Company

The top strategy tools being used by companies (out of 25 management tools) included;

- Benchmarking (#2 tool).
- Strategic Planning (#4).
- Balanced Scorecard (#6).
- Mission and Vision Statements (#7).
- Core Competencies (#11).
- Digital Transformation (#15).
- Strategic Alliances (#17).

# BENCHMARKING

Benchmarking at #2 is particularly popular with large companies. 44% of respondents (30,000 in total) according to the Bain research are using this tool. Benchmarking means that companies identify the best practices for operations and sales activities, and they compare their companies level of performance with other leading companies (what and how). The key element in benchmarking is to compare your company with companies who exhibit superior performance. Furthermore, it is essential to understand how those levels of performance were achieved (processes and practices) and which processes and practices is driving performance. Bench marking can also be done with companies outside of your industry (for example, Microsoft compares their product development processes with leading pharmaceutical R&D processes).

Based on the benchmarking analysis findings, companies then make every effort to improve their performance by adopting the best processes and practices identified. When adopting new practices/processes a company should always consider their unique business context. Companies use benchmarking exercises to;

- **Increase Performance**: Operational efficiency, product design, marketing, sales and more.
- **Assess Cost Competitiveness**: Cost comparisons are made with leading firms (relative cost position) and improvements made.
- **Enhance Strategic Advantage**: Mission critical capabilities which enhance performance are compared with other leading firms.

- **Improve Knowledge Creation and Learning**: New and novel processes and practices are identified and incorporated into the business.

The benchmarking process should be tailored to the strategic areas being investigated (operations, research etc.), and incorporate the following stages;

- Identify process, product or service area to be investigated (involve employees who will implement new processes in the future from the beginning of the process).
- Define the Key Performance Indicators (KPI's) which will be used for comparison purposes.
- Identify areas within the company to investigate, and the external companies who perform best on the KPI's selected (best practices).
- Monitor and collect data on the performance/practices of the KPI's selected (define and defend selection criteria).
- Compare and analyze results to identify relative performance and practices capabilities (define improvement priorities).
- Incorporate the best practices into the company's operations, monitor and evaluate the results over time.

## Strategic Planning

Companies use strategic planning to;

- Alter the direction and improve the performance of the business.
- Facilitate active discussion by top management on issues which are mission critical to the business.
- Construct a company-specific decision analysis framework (priorities).
- Establish a framework for resource allocation, budgeting and performance evaluations.
- Create an effective information gathering process which support decision making.
- Substantiate and validate decisions made and, the direction of the business overall.

The critical point to remember about strategic planning is that the planning process is more important than the outcome. This is the case because; the planning process enables company leaders to learn, define, compare and select smart alternatives. A Smart Strategic Planning Process includes;

- Defining Mission, Vision and Values.
- Targeting business segments and consider the threats/opportunities.
- Defining current and future priorities for the targeted segments.
- Determining the company's strengths/weaknesses relative to competitors. Make a value chain analysis (in-house vs. out-source activities).
- Evaluating different strategic alternatives.

- Engineering a business model which differentiates the firm from competitors. Define critical objectives for the business and consider stakeholder needs.
- Defining programs, plans and policies for implementing the strategy.
- Designing supportive organizational structures, decision processes, and information/control systems.
- Allocate resources to priority areas, and for developing capabilities.
- Create contingency plans to deal with unexpected events.
- Monitor and report performance.

## BALANCED SCORECARD

The Balanced Scorecard (BSC) process establishes concrete performance metrics and objectives for a company's strategy, which can be quantified and measured over time. The quantified metrics/objectives are based on a company's mission and vision (individualized for every company). Therefore, every company must create a unique and tailored BSC which address the following criteria;

- **Financial**: Revenues, earnings, ROC, cash flow etc.
- **Customer**: Market share, satisfaction, loyalty etc.
- **Internal Processes**: Productivity, quality, time efficiency etc.
- **Innovation**: Improvement index, employee input, new product launches (revenue contribution) etc.

- **Human Capital**: Employee engagement, turnover, development etc.

The BSC process is implemented in the following stages;

- Agree on the company's vision and mission (objectives).
    - Vision = the optimal desired future state (North Star).
    - Mission = the present state and purpose of the organization (what, who, and how).
- Define performance metrics which are directly linked to the achievement of the vision and mission (financial, operational, innovation, human), and are based on a pre-defined timeframe (short-term and long-term).
- Achieve organizational-wide understanding and adoption of the performance measures created. Those performance measures should be linked to; budgets, monitoring, communication and reward systems.
- Evaluate the data gathered from the monitoring processes (actual vs. desired).
- Take actions on areas which are under-performing, based on the criteria established in the earlier steps.

## Vision and Mission Statements

Mission and Vision statements are distinguished from each other as follows;

- **Vision Statement**: The desired optimal future state (North Star).
- **Mission Statement**: The purpose of the organization now (what, who, and how).

Vision and Mission statements are used to; identify and establish a company's culture, commitments, performance metrics, communication priorities, decision making practices, ethical standards, relationships with external stakeholders, and public relations message.

## Core Competencies (Capabilities)

Core competencies enable companies to produce and deliver unique value (strengths) to their customers. Core competencies are also based on a company's capability to coordinate, configure and integrate production, technologies and processes. Competencies can support a company when they are diversifying their areas of activity (diversification is based upon competencies rather than only industry characteristics and market segments). Competencies can also make a significant contribution to companies offering (value proposition). Critical core competencies should be hard for competitors to duplicate (or well protected to prevent others from adopting them). The process for identifying core competencies includes;

- Identifying company-wide capabilities which can and do have significant benefits for the company (processes, etc.).
- Benchmarking competencies with other best-in-practice companies.
- Selecting competencies which contribute the greatest added-value.
- Establishing competency-building capabilities in the organization.
- Support the critical competencies through external parties (alliances, licensing etc.), in order to strengthen those further.
- Establishing communication channels, and competency information sharing within the organization (leaning more about competencies).
- Maintaining and preserving the critical competencies, even when business activities change.
- Establishing organized abandonment processes to remove non-core capabilities (which are not adding significant value to the company).

## DIGITAL TRANSFORMATION

The rate of digital transformation is accelerating in all business (technology strategy). Therefore; digital agility capabilities are becoming increasingly important. Digital transformation in a company can support; the supply chain, customer engagement, data security, marketing analytics and more. Analytics have been rising quickly on the executive radar screen. This is because; effective analytics enable companies to gather insightful data from customers, along with helping to automate previously manual operations (resulting in faster decision making). Therefore, Big Data capabilities are becoming increasingly important for many company's strategic viability.

According to MIT research, most companies are concerned that the pace of change in their organizations is far too slow (63% of respondents). This slow pace of change is primarily due to the lack of urgency felt my management to change practices (enhance digital capabilities). The second reason for the lack of initiatives is the availability of adequate funding. These top two reasons are followed by; inadequate IT systems, unclear roles and responsibilities, and lack of company vision. The MIT research recommends that every company must;

- Develop a digitalization vision (how to engage customers and achieve profitable growth).
- Articulate (explain and document) that vision in an understandable way.
- Create a digitalization road-map (and commitment to the road-map).
- Establish measurable goals and rewards.

## STRATEGIC ALLIANCES

Alliances are established when two or more companies agree to combine their resources in order to achieve a common goal. Alliances may be formed for different purposes, and for different activities (customer, supplier, competitor etc.). Strategic alliances enable companies to improve their competitive standing in an industry, access new markets, enhance skills (competencies), share costs (economies of scale etc.), and lower the risks of doing business. Alliances may also allow companies to access new technologies, enhance research and development capabilities, improve quality, and deter competition. Alliances should only be established after a company has completed the following;

- Determined how the alliance can support the company's vision and mission.
- Identified and evaluated the potential partners who have the best-fit (synergy), and a workable business philosophy (cultural fit).
- Established an achievable, well-defined, and mutually beneficial contract (including agreed upon practices, policies etc.).
- Created a formal relationship including; pre-defined working practices, processes, reporting, accountability, and monitoring systems.

PwC have identified seven factors (steps), which help ensure that alliances are successful – maximize return on investment (ROI). Those seven factors are (in order of importance);

1. The alliance strategy should be created before seeking out alliance partners.
2. Joint-planning with alliance partners is necessary after their selection (trust building).
3. Establish formal terms and conditions (sharing of assets, people etc.) and end-of-alliance processes (pre-nuptial agreement).
4. Establish trust through; open, transparent, equitable, and fair terms and conditions.

5. Start small (achieve small objectives first), and only then expand as the level of trust and confidence grows.
6. Establish metrics for success, and track/report those metrics.
7. Establish an enterprise-wide alliance function (to share best practices, coordinate relationships, and establish a collaborative culture).

## SOURCES:

- Rigby, Darrell, and B. Bilodeau (2015). Management Tools and Trends 2015. Bain and Company
- Stauffer, David (2003). Best Practices for Benchmarking. Harvard Business School Working Knowledge
- Vanderbloeman, William (2016). Strategic Planning is Dead. Forbes
- Kaplan, Robert, and D. Norton (2007). Using the Balanced Scorecard as A Strategic Management System. Harvard Business Review
- Lagerstedt, Elisabeth (2014). Business Strategy: Are You inside-out or Outside-In. INSEAD Knowledge
- Fitzgerald, Michael, N. Kruschwitz, d. Bonnet, and M. Welch (2013). Embracing Digital Technology: A New Strategic Imperative. MIT Sloan Management Review
- McGahan, Greg (2016). Seven Factors for Successful Alliances and Joint Ventures. PwC

# TASK 6: Final Online Assessment

Let's Talk About Strategy has covered a broad range of topics which a very relevant for every existing and future manager. To reinforce you're learning, we recommend that you now complete the final online assessment.

LINK: Let's Talk About Strategy Final Assessment
https://goo.gl/RiNXhX

Note: The quiz requires 15+ minutes to complete


Please take the time to review Let's Talk About Strategy in order that others might learn from your experience.

LINK: Amazon.com Review Page
https://goo.gl/pgbJNy

**LINK: Amazon.uk Review Page**
https://goo.gl/1j6jP7

# CONCLUSION

*'Strategy = Knowing where you're going, why you're going there, how you're getting there, and what's different about how you're doing it'*

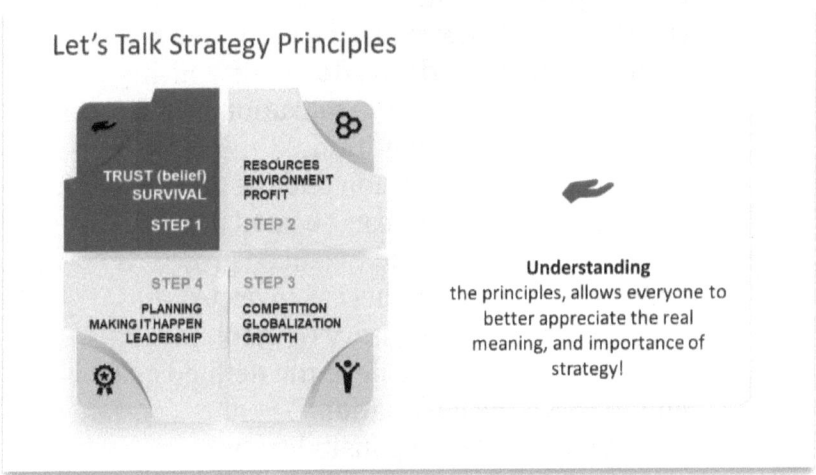

1. Trust does not guarantee success, but without it, business (and life) is a game of survival. High levels of trust help organizations move beyond survival.
2. Resources are necessary to move beyond survival. Without the necessary resources, organizations are like a car with no gasoline in the tank.
3. The environment determines how and if organizations need to adjust or adapt their resources.
4. Change is necessary and can be profitable (not changing can be deadly). When organizations are not ready to change, they become blind to

opportunities. Profit is the reward for positive change.
5. Competition brings profits. Fair competition is healthy and makes every organization stronger.
6. Globalization brings with it new players, new games (products and services), new playgrounds (markets) and new rules. However, the right strategy understands the demands which globalization present. Globalization is in fact just another form of competition.
7. Globalization, competition and the environment affect growth. Growth can be good and bad however; moderate and balanced growth is essential in order for success to occur.
8. Great planning is necessary to; implement a successful strategy, achieve the defined goals and to reach the destination.
9. Teamwork (roles, responsibility, and accountability) make strategy a reality.
10. Leaders must communicate every day… to everyone;
    - The important role all employees plays in executing strategy (the how)?
    - Where the company is going?
    - Why the company is going there?
    - How the company is getting there?
    - What's different about that how?
    - Commitment to trust?

Having now completed this purpose-driven strategy book, you have a much better understanding of strategy. With this understanding, you can now play a more important role in helping your company realize a brighter future (for everyone). Through a common understanding of strategy, you, your colleagues, and all employees in your organization will be getting closer and closer to; 'all that you desire to become'.

## PLEASE WRITE A REVIEW

If you found Let's Talk About Strategy to be of value, please write an Amazon customer review in order that others can also learn from your experience.

Review Link: Amazon.com
https://goo.gl/9Lssze

Review Link: Amazon.uk
https://goo.gl/1j6jP7

**View the author page on Amazon to see other books and videos on the topics covered.**

Author Page Link: Amazon.com
https://goo.gl/crbRua

Author Page Link: Amazon.uk
https://goo.gl/mVNPaJ

Kind regards and Thank You

Dr. Gerard L. Danford

# OTHER KINDLE BOOKS BY DR. GERARD DANFORD

**The Mini MBA Bootcamp:** Do you want to improve your chances of success in business without having to invest in an MBA? The business environment today is changing rapidly, and the time to develop ourselves is limited. Therefore, it is essential to focus on a limited number of high-value development goals that provide the highest return on investment (ROI). The Mini MBA Bootcamp delivers excellent value for your time. The Mini MBA Bootcamp does that by focusing on just 18 proven concepts which will make the greatest difference in your career.

Book Link: Amazon.com
https://goo.gl/FrLsPP

Book Link: Amazon.uk
https://goo.gl/piUzaS

# Strategy Vocabulary

## Glossary of Terms

|  |  |
|---|---|
| Acquisition | Taking control of a firms (51% or more) voting shares |
| Adaptive Strategy Style | Suitable in less predictable and faster moving environments |
| Asset Velocity | How efficiently company uses assets to generate revenue |
| Barriers to Entry | Economic, procedural, regulatory, or technological factors that prevent new firms from entering an industry |
| BCG Matrix | Compare business units against competitors based on: market growth and market share |
| Business Environment | Internal and external factors that influence a company's operating situation. |
| Business Model | The value proposition (customer), resources, processes and profit formula |
| Business Process Reengineering | Redesign of processes to achieve dramatic improvements in critical areas (cost, quality, service, and response time) |
| Capabilities | Ability to achieve objectives, in relation to overall mission |
| Classical Strategy Style | Suitable in predictable but hard to change environments |
| Competencies | Ability to perform, achieve, accomplish (may not have value) |
| Competitive Advantage | Provide same value as competitors but at lower price, or can charge higher prices (differentiation) |
| Competitive Strategy | Action plan to gain competitive advantage over rivals |
| Core Competency | the strengths or advantages including; knowledge and technical capacities etc. |
| Differentiation | Product (service, brand) that provides unique value to customers in comparison to competitors |
| Employee Engagement | Employees are; contributing (effort), committed, trusting, and stimulated; to achieve performance and company goals |
| Five Forces Model | External factors that affect viability of an industry: (new/existing competitors, substitute products, buyers, and suppliers |
| Four Strategic Styles | Classical, Adaptive, Shaping, and Visionary |
| Generic Strategies | Strategic planning that involves: differentiation, focus, and low cost |
| Globalization | Economic, financial, trade, and communication integration (interconnected and interdependent world) |
| Hierarchy | Pyramid of ranking individuals, authority, importance, and influence |
| Implementation | The process of putting a decision or plan into effect; execution |

|  |  |
|---|---|
| Innovation | Translating idea or invention into goods or services that create value |
| Integration | Achieving close/seamless coordination between systems, people, processes and organizations |
| Interdependence | Dependence of entities (departments, companies etc.) on each other |
| Key Performance Indicator | Firm's critical performance indicators (KPI), shows progress (or lack of it) towards realizing objectives |
| Maslow Hierarchy | The 5 different needs that motivate human behavior |
| Merger | Combining two firms into one new legal entity |
| Mission | The present state and purpose of the organization (what, who, and how) |
| Net Income | Total revenue minus all expenses during the same period |
| Operational Budgets | Anticipated material and labor costs needed to run the business and to manufacture products or provide services. |
| Organizational Agility | Capability to rapidly change or adapt in response to changes in the market |
| Profit | The surplus remaining after total costs are deducted from total revenue |
| Purpose | The reason for being, what the organization stands for in historical, ethical, emotional and practical terms |
| Resource Allocation | Where, when and how to use available resources (human, capital) |
| Return of Capital | Profitability of firm (% of funds acquired from investors and lenders) ROC |
| Return on Assets | Ability to efficiently allocate and manage resource (ROA) |
| Return on Investment | Ratio of net income (profit less depreciation) to average capital employed |
| S&P 500 | Benchmark indicator of the overall US stock market performance |
| Scale (economies) | Cost advantage that arises with increased output |
| Shaping Strategy Style | Suitable in less predictable but workable environments |
| Strategic Planning | Envisioning desired future, defining goals, objectives and steps |
| Strategy | Where were going, why, how and what's different about our strategy |
| Survival Rate | Percentage of companies still active after a given period of time |
| Sustainable Advantage | Long-term competitive advantage that is not easily duplicated by competitors |
| Transformation | Radical organization change (new direction and new level of effectiveness) |
| Vision | The optimal desired future state (North Star) |
| Visionary Strategy Style | Suitable in more predictable and workable environments |
| Zero Based Budgeting | Cash flow budgets and operating plans which every year must start from scratch with no pre-authorized funds |

www.ingramcontent.com/pod-product-compliance
Lightning Source LLC
Chambersburg PA
CBHW020923180526
45163CB00007B/2856